COMBAT
TRAUMA

Alan,

Cos I have told you many times, you are one of my heroes.

Hope this book is of interest and value to you.

Charlie Taylor

COMBAT TRAUMA

A Personal Look at Long-Term Consequences

James D. Johnson

Rowman & Littlefield Publishers, Inc.
Lanham • Boulder • New York • Toronto • Plymouth, UK

Published by Rowman & Littlefield Publishers, Inc.
A wholly owned subsidiary of The Rowman & Littlefield Publishing Group, Inc.
4501 Forbes Boulevard, Suite 200, Lanham, Maryland 20706
www.rowman.com

10 Thornbury Road, Plymouth PL6 7PP, United Kingdom

British Library Cataloguing in Publication Information Available

Library of Congress Cataloging-in-Publication Data

The hardback edition of this book was previously cataloged by the Library of
Congress as follows:

Johnson, James, 1940–
  Combat trauma : a personal look at long-term consequences / James D.
Johnson.
    p. cm.
  Includes index.
  1. War neuroses. 2. Post-traumatic stress disorder. I. Title.
  RC550.J66 2010
  616.85'212—dc22   2010004774

ISBN: 978-1-4422-0434-8 (cloth : alk. paper)
ISBN: 978-1-4422-0435-5 (pbk. : alk. paper)
ISBN: 978-1-4422-0436-2 (electronic)

Printed in the United States of America

We express profound appreciation to those who have loved, tolerated, and nurtured us when our behaviors were not understood, even to ourselves. Our spouses, children, friends, and work associates have often seen our exterior but only brief glimpses of the puzzling hidden inner feelings and memories resulting from combat violence so many years ago. Without you, life would have remained empty and meaningless. Thank you!

FORTY YEARS AGO

Excerpt from poem by Denny Tuttle
199th Light Infantry Brigade, Vietnam

Once we were young and once we were strong,
And we were sent to a war where we didn't belong.
We did our time and saw men die
And it changed our lives forever, both you and I . . .

Most of us came home but not all, as you know,
And there is a memorial for them, if by chance you should go.
They didn't get a chance to live their lives,
And so many left behind both children and wives.

Just forget that old war, our Uncle Sam said.
Easier said than done, especially when lying in bed.
Many of us got spit on when we came back,
Unlike today's soldiers coming from Iraq . . .

We have tried to live normal and overcome the past,
But the memories of that war will forever last.
Some have done well with lives that are now rich,
While others have fallen and ended up in a ditch . . .

No one can understand what that war did to so many;
Should have walked a mile in our shoes for a reason, if any.
People never understood us I can honestly say,
Because they weren't there, Lord how could they?

We have passed through these years with not much to say,
But remembering that time we spent, day by day.
Our time has about run out now to start over again,
Because we'll all be leaving here, we just don't know when.

Many have died in the years that have passed
At peace with their maker and free at last.
We hope that someday all will learn what they need to know,
About the men who fought a war some "Forty Years Ago."

CONTENTS

1

THEN AND NOW

The squishing sound is like a knife opening a cold watermelon. Except the sharp steel that cuts into a tasty melon is nothing like the metal that just came from somewhere in the tree line a hundred or so meters to my left. I know immediately that it is the metal from an enemy AK-47 rifle.

The round enters just above my left rib cage and exits just below and slightly to the right of my right nipple. In a nanosecond, my mind is flooded with thousands of thoughts. I instinctively place my left palm over the exit wound and can feel only warm blood and what seems like the insides of a melon, dangling down my side toward my spine.

I am crumpled on my right side, afraid to move for fear that my insides will indeed fall out the lemon-sized hole in my side. Why am I even conscious? Or alive? Did this round not tear into my heart? I can still breathe, albeit I am breathing hard, like an Olympic runner just finishing a four-hundred-meter race.

I know I must have help immediately, else I will bleed to death. My mind is surprisingly clear, and I know I am on the top side of an armored troop carrier (ATC), a specially designed sixty-foot navy boat ferrying a platoon of infantry into a combat operational objective in the Mekong Delta. I also know this is one of fifteen boats loaded with three of our infantry companies.

As usual, we had loaded at 2:00 a.m. and traveled on the small stream until first light. I had just climbed the few feet above the well deck of the boat to observe the beautiful sunrise over the lush Vietnam foliage when the round tore into me. I am lying crumpled on the platform just a few feet from the infantrymen just below me. Strangely, I want to curse myself for allowing myself to be exposed to an unseen enemy gunner while indulging in the luxury of watching the sunrise. I should have stayed the few feet below in the relative safety of the well deck of the boat, where small-arms fire could not penetrate.

I feel panic. I try to yell out that I am hit, but I hear only my feeble gurgling deep in my throat, which is filling with blood. My beloved infantrymen just feet below deck are like they are miles away. Maybe they, like me, never heard the shot that tore through my body. I surmise that my blood will soon drain and drip onto them below. Where is the medic? I am petrified that I am dying—yet I still feel no pain, only panic.

I try to turn over and get out of the sights of the Viet Cong who have just shot me, but I cannot move. My legs will not work. I force my right hand to feel other parts of my body to determine if I am hit anywhere else. I feel warm moisture but am unsure if this is blood or perspiration.

Both banks of the 150-foot-wide stream now become like Mount St. Helens as they explode with enemy fire. Explosions are occurring on several boats ahead. I have an unobstructed view of three raging fires on board and hear our heavy weapons returning fire toward the dug-in enemy.

I have no relief because I am still crumpled in full sight of what appear to be hordes of bunker-protected enemy who are firing at will at our very exposed boats loaded with infantrymen. I hear orders being yelled into radios as well as screams from nearby boats, apparently of others who are being wounded in the ambush. Sounds of small-arms fire now are whizzing by very close. I still cannot move and no one has come to my assistance. My mind is on fire as I fear that any second, another enemy round will rip into my body and finish me off. I am helpless to take protective cover from the increasing enemy fire. Nor do I have a weapon to defend myself.

Visions of my beautiful wife, Barbara, and my two-and-a-half-year-old daughter and ten-month-old son, Kellie and Grey, flash through my mind. I will never see or hold any of them again! The melting pot of fear, hurt, and anger supersede the now-increasing pain from the gunshot. I have seen many other infantrymen shot, and when a round tore through their skin, muscle, and bones, pain was usually very pronounced.

It seems like hours, but I know it is probably only minutes into the huge battle raging all up and down the stream—and I am still exposed and cannot move! Objects begin to blur, as it seems the early morning fog is mixing with smoke from explosions and the three fires on the nearby boats.

Suddenly I am aware of darkness, as if another round has hit the vision center in the back of my brain. Am I passing out? I see murky shadows on the walls, obviously from nearby streetlights. How can that be? God, I am in the midst of another furious firefight—not at home! My mind is on overload. I am sweating profusely. My legs are moving but I am not going anywhere. I am hollering for help. I am trying to crawl to safety but I get tangled up in the blanket. For God's sake, where did that blanket and sheet come from? No one even knows I have been hit. Have I passed out and a medic has finally covered me? Am I being evacuated on a chopper to safety? The sun was just coming up, so I know it is not dark.

Miraculously, my wife is still asleep. My wife? Where the dickens am I? How can that be? My racing mind is fibrillating from the firefight in the Mekong Delta to my bedroom, from extreme fear to disbelief that I am in my bed. I feel my right side to see if any of my insides have extricated themselves as a result of the bullet. I feel only sweat.

I should feel relief that maybe, just maybe, this was only a nightmare. But in the twilight of early morning, I take no solace in the fact that possibly it is a dream. It couldn't be. It is too real. I felt the bullet. I felt the blood as my palm was blocking my insides from exiting from the wound. I heard and saw the sounds of the battle, like I have dozens of times.

Trembling, I sit on the side of my bed. My mind is still not clear. I am still not totally sure what is real. Am I going into a coma from the gunshot and, in my unconsciousness, it just appears that I am back home? Or was this just a nightmare like I have had hundreds of times before, about the sheer terror of combat?

I rise unsteadily to my feet. I don't want to awaken my wife—it's not fair to her. Plus, I am now a bit embarrassed—if it is a nightmare, why can't I seem to control their occurrences?

I step into the bathroom. The bubbling sound of my pee hitting the water serves as a wake-up call. By the time I have emptied my bladder, I know it was another of those horrible nightmares. I am relieved, yet angry that now, four decades later, I am still in Vietnam, and I realize I will never be totally out of combat.

I sigh and realize that this is another event I will discuss with my VA therapist during my next appointment. I just woke up, yet I am drained of energy.

I know that my post-traumatic stress disorder (PTSD) is a lifetime sentence. I tell others it will only be cured if I get Alzheimer's disease. Yet, I am not sure that even that dreaded disease would remove the intrusive memories and unanticipated feelings that have haunted hundreds of thousands of combat troops in the past as well as the present.

The terror and trauma of combat invades our souls with a "till death do us part" sentence from which no divorce is possible. Those of us who were exposed to the continual violence of combat live with nightmares, flashbacks, sleep problems, triggers that take us back to combat, isolation, depression, sadness, anger, guilt, denial, and many other symptoms of our unseen wounds from our traumas.

Yes, our traumas were four decades ago. Someone may ask, "When were you in Vietnam?" An easy answer for many of us is "Last night."

The sixteen of us who have collaborated on this book take no immediate comfort in making ourselves transparent by revealing our innermost thoughts and feelings that originate from our horrible days in combat. However, our research indicates that much has been written about combat trauma, but most has been written by clinicians and/or by one person. Nowhere have we found a group of combat veterans such as the sixteen of us collaborating in telling the collective story of what constant exposure to the terror and horror of combat does to a person over a lifetime.

Much denial exists about the lingering effects of combat trauma. This denial was poignantly illustrated a number of years ago by George C. Scott, who played the role of General Patton in the movie *Patton*. He illustrated profanely and perfectly the condescending reaction of many in past decades to those with psychological injuries resulting from combat. Visiting the aid station behind the front lines, Patton came upon a soldier sitting on the edge of his hospital bed. Seeing no visible signs of wounds, Patton asked, "What's wrong with you, son?" The young soldier stammered, somewhat awed by the presence of a general, and obviously did not know how to answer the question. Impatient, Patton yelled, "So what the h--- is your problem, soldier?" The nursing attendant accompanying the general answered, "Sir, he is suffering from combat fatigue." Becoming hysterical, Patton screamed, "Combat fatigue? Combat fatigue!? Why, you're nothing but a g-- d--- coward! A coward!! Look at these other bastards here who are wounded, and you, you son-of-a-bitch, are just sitting here like you're one of them! You're nothing but a f------ coward." With that, a raging Patton hit the soldier with his gloves and stormed out of the aid station.

Even though this ignorant tirade cost Patton his command, it nevertheless illustrates the prevailing attitude that if there is no blood, there is no harm. Even though this attitude is gradually changing, the journeys of the sixteen of us deal with our unseen wounds. In fact, there have been articles recently about a two-star and a four-star general who have sought help for their PTSD symptoms.

Hundreds of thousands of combat veterans have nightmares and suffer numerous other debilitating symptoms of combat trauma. Indications are that the veterans of the first Persian Gulf War and more recently those from Iraq and Afghanistan are having significant problems with PTSD. Recent media coverage has brought to light some of the many problems associated with the aftereffects of combat trauma. Suicide rates in the military are increasing dramatically. Still, treatment at some of the medical facilities has gotten a lot of negative press.

It is our hope that in reading about some of our struggles over the past four decades, others may identify and know that they are not alone, and that they can learn to manage the symptoms of PTSD and not have the symptoms rule their life.

2

WE SIXTEEN—WHO WE ARE

As very young men, we all hugged and kissed our loved ones good-bye, and we went off to experience more violence and combat trauma in a very short period of time than a thousand civilians will experience in a lifetime. The effects of this trauma are still with each of us now, four decades later.

The sixteen of us went into combat, returned, and for the most part, were and are very typical Americans. We have raised our families, had careers, and tried to live normal lives. Each of us, though, has been and is living two lives. One is what the public sees, which may appear quite normal. The other, however, is deeply embedded in our souls, which are feelings and behaviors. It has been and is difficult to reveal them, but they now are seen in our writings.

When the idea of this project originated, I realized that for there to be credibility, it was necessary to have credible combat veterans tell their stories. I personally invited each of these brothers to be a part of this project. I personally know each of these veterans and know of their integrity, character, and history. In short, I trust each of these combat brothers today because I trusted them four decades ago with my life.

Let us introduce ourselves.

John Adame: Whittier, California. Born of Mexican immigrant parents, John grew up in East Los Angeles. As a youngster, he found his identity as a runner. He was drafted and served as a rifleman and radio operator in E/3/60th Infantry. Had a career in the U.S. Postal Service before having to retire.

Terry Gander: Grew up and still lives in Evansville, Indiana. Was very poor; his family had no indoor plumbing until he was in high school. Drafted and served as rifleman in B/3/60th Infantry. Had a career with a steel company and Alcoa Aluminum prior to having to retire.

John Iannucci: Asheville, North Carolina. Grandparents were Italian immigrants. John grew up in Staten Island, New York. Volunteered for the draft and served as a rifleman in B/3/60th Infantry. For the first seven months in daily combat, John received no pay because his "records were messed up." For over three decades he has owned a very successful Italian restaurant in Skyland, North Carolina.

James D. (Jim) Johnson: Fayetteville, North Carolina. Grew up in Albemarle, North Carolina. Like Terry, he grew up poor, had no indoor plumbing until half grown. Decided early that God was calling him to be a minister. Became an all-state tackle on a state championship team, which enabled him to get a college scholarship. Battalion Chaplain, 3/60th Infantry. Never carried a weapon in combat. Spent twenty years in the army, and then was a therapist/pastoral counselor for fifteen years before having to retire.

Frank Martinolich: Olympia, Washington. Grew up in Lacey, Washington. Was one of seven children. Made money by picking strawberries and selling newspapers. Developed into a skilled baseball player and was ready to sign a professional contract when he was drafted. Served as rifleman and radio operator in A/3/60th Infantry. Worked thirty years as a production worker and shop steward and is now retired.

Ron Miriello: Sanford, North Carolina. Grew up in Shomokin and Mt. Carmel, Pennsylvania, and Erwin, North Carolina. As a youngster, he accidentally slipped into a whirlpool in the dangerous Cape Fear River and was pulled unconscious from the water. Enlisted in the navy and became a "River Rat." Fifty-cal machine gunner on an armored troop carrier (ATC) and then on an assault support patrol boat. Retired as vice president of Central Carolina Community College.

Guy P. Moore: Detroit, Michigan. Grew up in California, Arizona, New York, and Michigan. Began flying lessons at fifteen, soloed at sixteen, and intended to get his pilot's license but the draft interrupted his dream. Served as rifleman and radio operator with B/3/60th Infantry. Because of so many dangerous flights in combat, lost the desire to fly. Worked with Ford Motor Company prior to having to retire.

Roy Moseman: Grew up and still lives in Athens, Georgia. Was born in the projects, moved across the street, and even though living in the city, raised rabbits, chickens, and goats. Volunteered for the draft and served as a rifleman, radio operator, squad leader, and platoon sergeant with C/4/47th Infantry. Owned Classic Electrical Contracting prior to having to retire.

Bob Nichols: Campobello, South Carolina. Grew up in Belfast, New York. Played soccer; was in band, choir, and a drum and bugle corps; and was senior class president. Painted his first house at thirteen and by sixteen had a business painting houses, in addition to working for farmers. Rifleman and radio operator with B/3/60th Infantry. Retired after thirty-three years as distribution officer, Rochester Gas and Electric Co.

Tony Normand: Fayetteville, North Carolina. Grew up in central Alabama. Poor and son of a Baptist pastor. Had to work as a youngster and later became student body president of his university. Served as a platoon leader and then as a company commander of C/5/60th Mechanized Infantry. Retired after thirty years in the army and was the chief of staff of Special Operations Command, Fort Bragg. Now is CEO, Carolina Commerce and Technology Center, near Lumberton, North Carolina.

Mitch Perdue: North Augusta, South Carolina. Grew up in Newberry, South Carolina. Father committed suicide when Mitch was five. At fourteen, in effect was the family "father" and had to go to work in a cotton mill on third shift in order for his mother and two sisters to eat. Went to high school during the day. Drafted and served as a rifleman B/3/60th Infantry. After college, had a career as purchasing manager in the lumber business before having to retire.

Dave Schoenian: Grew up and still lives in Glen Dale, West Virginia. As an only child, he was raised by his grandparents. Loved playing little league and church league sports. Drafted and served as a rifleman, squad leader, and platoon sergeant with C/4/47th Infantry. Worked with a power company prior to having to retire.

Ray Shurling: Fayetteville, North Carolina. Grew up in small town of Perry, Georgia. Spent much time with his beloved grandfather in the country learning to fish, hunt, grow vegetables, and how to treat other people. Enlisted and served with a Special Forces unit. Adviser to a Vietnamese unit. Worked with Western Publishing Co. and now owns Cape Fear Distribution, Inc.

Bob Stumpf: Dingmans Ferry, Pennsylvania. Grew up in the Bronx, New York. One of five kids, slept in bunk beds, played stick ball in the streets, and sold newspapers. Spent five summers at a boys' camp that emphasized religion, sports, and military. Drafted and served as a rifleman with E/3/60th Infantry. Second Vietnam tour with 716 MP Battalion. Vice president with Israeli Discount Bank of New York before having to retire.

Charlie Taylor: Skull Valley, Arizona. Grew up in northern Arizona, developed a love of fishing and hunting. Was high school and college football player. Served as platoon leader and company commander of C/5/60th Mechanized Infantry. Senior Partner with Taylor and Padgett Financial Services in Prescott, Arizona, where he manages more than a hundred million dollars for clients.

Erol Tuzcu: Delray Beach, Florida. Grew up in Turkey, immigrated at age eighteen, and was barely able to speak English. Did not even know what television was until he arrived in the States. Worked as stockboy and was so poor he lived on Corn Flakes for weeks at a time. Was drafted a year after arriving in the United States. Served as a rifleman and later as a radio operator with A/3/60th Infantry. Owns U.S. Truss, Inc., in West Palm Beach, Florida.

So, who are we? We consist of two infantry officers, one chaplain, one navy River Rat, one Special Forces sergeant, and eleven infantrymen. Fifteen of us served with the famous Mobile Riverine Force in the Mekong Delta, and fourteen of us were with the Ninth Infantry Division (two of whom served with C/5/60th Mechanized Infantry, two with C/4/47th Infantry, ten with 3/60th Infantry), and one was a navy River Rat.

Each of us has a *public persona* that reflects success since our combat trauma. We have raised families and have tried to be good citizens. All of us have had successful careers since Vietnam, in spite of having been emotionally infected by the trauma we experienced. It is important that one not get the image that our lives have been all bad or that our personalities have been totally wrecked. In spite of the psychological damage from combat exposure, each of us has varying degrees of joy, happiness, and a sense that life really is good and worth living. In most ways, we all are very typical Americans.

The pain of our stories from combat trauma began as youngsters right out of school. When we were ordered into military service, our first humiliation was having to strip at the induction center in front of everyone, spreading our "cheeks" for the doctor to examine. We then were sent to be trained as killers, ordered into combat, and exposed to hellish trauma almost daily until we were wounded or had served out our tour. While our peers back home were going fishing, going to fraternity parties, going to the beach, and living "normal" lives growing up, we were seeing and doing violence that was horrifying and gruesome.

We have seen buddies with limbs blown off, entrails exiting from open wounds, and brain matter coming from where an ear once was. We have stuffed dead bodies into ponchos, hoping we included all the mud- and blood-covered body parts. As a result, each of us experienced horror, disbelief at the amount of combat destruction, paralyzing fear, unresolved and un-dealt-with grief, and countless other disarming emotions.

We went into combat with zest and vigor and left feeling like old men. Being constantly face to face with so much death, destruction, and violence resulted in fear, grief, horror, anger, disbelief, flashbacks, nightmares, emotional numbness, and dozens of other symptoms. We were changed forever.

What we experienced in combat is only a small part of our story, as this is *not* intended as a combat memoir. Rather, what has happened to us over the *following four decades* is, we believe, a story that much needs to be shared and heard. Much has been written and filmed about combat. Little has been written about the unseen wounds of combat— wounds to the heart, soul, and spirit of young, and now old, soldiers.

Imagine gasoline being thrown on you and a match igniting it and burning your body. During recovery and after, the wounds and scars are clearly visible to others. Now imagine being severely shocked from a live electrical wire. As the electricity enters the body, internal organs are burned and seared, but on the outside you appear to be unscathed. The difference is that your wounds are all out of sight and on the inside.

An observer has no way to know the degree of internal wounds. So it is that emotional wounds are deep inside and are invisible to others. Most of us have intentionally kept them there for four decades.

In sports, the more one conditions his or her body with strenuous exercise and practice drills, the greater the chance of success and the less chance of injury. No so with trauma. The greater the exposure to traumatic events, the greater the likelihood that psychological injury will occur.

The prolonged exposure to combat gradually wore us down, and many of us have remained emotionally exhausted for decades. In some ways we have been left in perpetual emotional limbo. Each of us also has an *unseen side*, a life sentence of trauma symptoms that most others, even our families and close friends, may not even know exists.

Fourteen of us have been diagnosed by the Veterans Administration with PTSD and have had individual and/or group therapy. Additionally, five of us have received inpatient treatment for PTSD and related disorders. Ten of us are totally retired due to the effects of our combat trauma, and some of us are now rated by the VA as Individual Unemployable due to our combat-related conditions.

Being diagnosed with PTSD is simply an explanation of an unseen combat wound. It is *not* a license to run wild, insult others, avoid responsibilities, or treat loved ones with unkindness and disrespect. Feelings? Yes. Bad behaviors? No.

Several sets of circumstances bind us all together. First, we were all in dozens of acts of combat violence. Second, many of us served together or were in the same unit. Third, we all were profoundly affected by our combat trauma and it still very much affects each of us four decades later. Fourth, being under fire has bonded us together as brothers— blood brothers in a literal sense of the word.

By military standards, we all succeeded in doing our jobs in Vietnam. Combat awards and decorations are relative with us. Just getting home alive for most of us was award enough. Nevertheless, collectively we received the following combat awards:

Silver Star: 2
Purple Heart: 18
Bronze Star: 12
Air Medal: 24

Soldiers Medal: 1
Army Commendation Medal for Valor: 8
Combat Infantryman Badge: 14
Presidential Unit citations: 16
Navy Achievement Medal with "V" for Valor: 1

Additionally, paperwork was submitted but lost for one Silver Star, three Purple Hearts, three Bronze Stars, one Air Medal, and one Army Commendation Medal.

Why, then, four decades after the last shot was fired at us, do we now have a desire to reveal our deep emotional wounds? *Why* are we willing to make ourselves transparent by exposing very personal thoughts, feelings, and behaviors? *Why* are we willing to take the risk, especially knowing that what many of us are sharing may not be known even by our best friends and loved ones?

First, tens of thousands of combat veterans are trapped in their past and do not know what to do with their bottled-up feelings. We want them to know that they are not alone and that there are healthy ways to avoid keeping their bottles so tight.

Second, family members and friends of these thousands see and live with the results of their combat trauma and may not even know it. Plus, the common thread of the trauma victim "never talking about it" is puzzling. We hope that by sharing our stories, more can be understood about the effects of trauma.

Third, so little has been understood by the American public about the aftereffects of combat trauma, even though almost weekly there are news reports talking about PTSD. Very little is known about how it manifests in everyday life and especially for decades after combat.

Fourth, it has been thought that combat trauma symptoms are simply a mental illness. Maybe they are, but first, for sure, they are combat wounds. We want our stories to be understood for what they are— wounds to the soul and spirit of combat soldiers and sailors.

Fifth, the compilation of our stories hopefully will be a resource for clinical providers who attempt to treat the victims of trauma.

Sixth, it is hoped that national leaders who consider sending young Americans into combat will know that the dangers are not just from combat itself but that lingering wounds to the soul usually remain for a lifetime—and not only do they affect the combat veteran but they can infect all who are around him or her.

Seventh, numerous troops are returning from Afghanistan and Iraq who are experiencing the effects of combat trauma. It goes without saying that each series of combat experiences is unique, from Iraq/Afghanistan to the Mekong Delta to Korea and World War II. However, the results of combat trauma can be the same.

Eighth, even though our victimization and stories are from combat, we are aware that many others have been victims of trauma from childhood abuse, rape, wrecks, being robbed at gunpoint, being physically attacked, natural and manmade disasters, and countless other trauma events. The symptoms of PTSD are the same, regardless of the source.

Resistance is still felt in many quarters that think only the weak have trouble. We know that this is faulty thinking. We hope that by revealing our struggles over the years, many of these newer combat veterans will realize that being wounded in their souls needs to be acknowledged and treated and that there is help available for them. There is no need for them to spend years and decades fighting their combat trauma alone.

Be assured that compiling our stories has in itself been somewhat traumatic. In reading the first draft, Guy P. Moore said, "Just reflecting on what we have put together is bringing tears to my eyes." Bob Nichols, reading the draft in his living room, said, "I had to leave the room and read elsewhere because I was not yet ready for my wife to see me crying." Ray Shurling said, "I have laid bare much of what has been kept hidden for almost forty years and it causes my brain to go on 'emotional alert.' I cannot read what we have written without tears."

Some of our traumatic memories and what they have done to us is very ugly and alarming. Yet we have attempted to "tell it like it is." Our stories are intentionally not clinical. Plenty of clinical material on combat trauma is available in writings by clinicians, in *The Diagnostic and Statistical Manual IV* (DSM IV), and in other documents, and we have no need to replicate them.

However, nothing has been written in the first person by a group of credible combat veterans from many walks of life like us who have lived with our symptoms for forty years. It is our desire that other victims and family members of trauma can identify with the personal stories of our life's journey in ways that will be insightful, affirming, healing, and hopeful.

The fact that we are willing and able to risk telling a part of our stories is in itself miraculous. However, we could not have told our individual stories alone because many would find unbelievable the details of the aftermath of combat trauma. In Vietnam, there was safety in numbers, as one would never go on a combat patrol alone. Likewise, we tell our stories in the safety of a supportive group of sixteen.

These introductions of who we are will be magnified greatly in the following stories of what happened to us in combat. What we have gone through was almost unbearable to each of us. Even more important is what we did with the effects of our combat trauma after we left Vietnam. We do not ask for sympathy for what we experienced then and now. We do ask for understanding—not so much for the sixteen of us, but for the hundreds of thousands of combat veterans of all wars who have been traumatized and live in every city, town, and hamlet of the United States, many if not most living with their painful secrets and unseen emotional wounds carefully tucked deep inside their souls.

Our stories are very raw. Blood, guts, and emotional gore can be described only in frank and uncensored language. Much of our stories could be X-rated based on the violence that we experienced and our reactions over the ensuing years.

There is a parable about when God was creating the model of a Vietnam combat veteran:

The Angel slowly ran his finger across the Vet's cheek and said, "Lord, there is a leak."
God said, "That's not a leak, that's a tear."
"What's the tear for. . .?" asked the Angel.
"It's for the bottled-up emotions, for holding fallen soldiers as they die, for commitment to the American flag, for the terror of living with PTSD for decades after the war, alone with its demons with no one to care or help."
"You're a genius," said the Angel, casting a gaze at the tear.
The Lord said, "I didn't put it there."[1]

---

[1] By Bob Scheyer © 1989 (adapted from the original written by Erma Bombeck).

Finally, not one of us will pocket a dime for publication of our stories. One hundred percent of advances and royalties, less literary agent commissions, will be donated to help other combat veterans.

So, we sixteen are making ourselves transparent so that maybe, just maybe, as a result of our stories, the public will better understand what happens when we send young men and women into combat.

I

GOING TO THE HELL OF COMBAT

Again, combat stories are not meant to be the central theme of these writings; rather our intent is to make transparent the *results* of combat and how combat trauma has impacted and changed our lives over the past four decades. However, it is impossible for the impact of combat trauma on our lives to be understood without demonstrated links to the actual horror of the combat itself. Therefore, we reveal a very small portion of our combat experiences.

3

OUR TRAUMAS

Stories abounded at stateside posts about Vietnam. But when we left the United States for Vietnam, there was no way any of us could have possibly been adequately prepared for the trauma about to be served to us.

Most feared by the combat soldier is walking into an ambush or being captured. Everyone is hyperalert for any indication of enemy presence; a smell, noise, or movement could be enough to raise an already elevated and overloaded mind. When the first shot is fired in any engagement with the enemy, the stakes are life or death. At that moment, we are not fighting for the United States, trying to take out world evil, or trying to free the Vietnamese people. We aren't fighting for ideals, love of country, or any Rambo type of myth. We are simply trying to keep from getting killed. To neutralize an ambush, it is necessary for us to overpower the enemy, which means throwing every bit of firepower possible at the suspected enemy positions. Not to do so could mean taking our last breath.

Our body reacts with adrenaline, pushing muscles and feelings beyond anything a civilian can possibly imagine. Life depends on our reaction as well as the actions of our brothers. When we stare down the barrel of an enemy machine gun firing at us, blood pressure rises dramatically, the heart pounds almost out of our chest, and our mind is instantly overloaded. Survival instinct means "kill the enemy before he kills me." Values, faith, or love of family are not in that instant a part of one's reaction. Rather, it is reacting as an animal being attacked, for we killed to protect one another and ourselves.

After the ambush and the firefight, stuffing the remains of a buddy into a poncho tears holes in the heart that last a lifetime. Being on the receiving end of enemy weapons never prepares you for the next time.

Misery of every kind imaginable was present on our combat operations, with the worst being the loss of your friends via death or injury. John Iannucci describes our combat trauma environment as follows:

> Every day, we battled the fear of hearing the sounds of the beginning of an ambush, the click of a booby trap, seeing something that would make you freeze and not react and maybe endanger the men around you, of the night, combat helicopter assaults into hot landing zones, night ambushes, observation posts, walking point, checking bunkers, snipers, punji pits, jammed weapons, running out of ammunition, B-40 rockets, rocket-propelled grenades (RPGs), mortar attacks, crawling through unforgiving knee-deep mud with gunfire everywhere, trying to reach wounded buddies lying in the open rice paddies, being killed or severely wounded—and the worst fear was being captured.
>
> The one hundred–degree heat was numbing with a seventy-pound rucksack strapped to your back. There were the leeches, snakes, mosquitoes, ringworm, malaria, stream crossings, heat stroke, exhaustion, immersion foot, sleep deprivation, hot canteen water, bad cigarettes, and C rations, all while never knowing if in the next second I would be wounded or killed. Then, after a battle, loading the blood- and mud-covered bodies of our dead brothers like logs onto a chopper and having no time to grieve over their massacred lives.

Frank Martinolich describes combat trauma like this:

> Walking point, alone, setting up three-man listening/observation posts one-hundred-plus yards in front of the rest of the unit, being shot at, being caught in an ambush and having guys die next to you and being helpless to do anything for them, having a buddy die in my arms because there are too many wounds to treat, or having to pick up pieces of a buddy who has just been blown in half.

Bob Stumpf says,

> We spent days humping through the jungle, crossing open rice paddies,
> canals, being constantly wet and burning up during the day and wet and
> cold at night. We had to deal with the mud, heat, humidity, mosquitoes,
> red ants, leeches, and the constant odor of rotting vegetation. It was hor-
> rible enough just dealing with the environment, let alone being in such
> peril and wondering if you would see tomorrow.

Words can give only a small part of what it is like to be in the midst of
a firefight in these conditions. Multiply many times the following stories
and the reader can still only imagine what it is like for a young troop to
experience the soul-shattering impact of a firefight. All of the vignettes
are very bloody and all are still heart-wrenching to us now, four decades
after the fact. For illustration purposes, we offer the following three
battles, which involved several of us. Many more could be given. Later
in our stories, other vignettes are included to illustrate what combat
trauma has done to us.

SNOOPY'S NOSE—SEPTEMBER 15, 1967

At exactly 7:30 a.m., all hell breaks loose. Alpha and Bravo companies
3/60th and Charlie 5/60th are aboard twelve navy ATCs accompanied
by a mine sweeper, four heavily armored "Monitors," a command and
control vessel, and a medical aid boat. Each boat is sixty feet long. Man-
ning the boats are the navy River Rat sailors.

On a small stream no more than 150 feet wide, the enemy opens up
on the convoy from heavily dug-in positions on both sides of the small
stream. This battle is described in my book, *Combat Chaplain: A Thirty-
Year Vietnam Battle*, as follows:

> The unmistakable rip of enemy AK-47 assault rifle fire, and the staccato
> sound of machine gun fire are interrupted time and time again by the
> explosions of rocket propelled grenades, recoilless rifles, and B-40 rock-
> ets. The Navy boats return massive amounts of fire onto the banks of the
> stream and the infantry soldiers fire from over the top of the well decks
> of their boats. When a River Rat is hit, an infantryman jumps into the gun
> turret and resumes firing.

Terry Gander is firing a machine gun over the side of his boat and catches a piece of enemy steel that penetrates his flak jacket and embeds in his chest. Terry's buddy, Kenny Lancaster, catches Terry as he collapses, easing him to the well deck floor. As a medic patches up Terry, Kenny takes over the machine gun and continues to fire.

Every boat is hit over and over and we are taking many casualties. A navy River Rat is in a pool of blood with his foot and the lower part of his left leg blown off. Chaos is all over the stream. Three boats are ablaze. Some boats slam into other boats by accident, as the sounds of battle are deafening and the haze from gunpowder hanging low over the water obscures clear vision. One wounded brother is wedged between the well deck and a stationary weapon, with an ashen-colored face and lifeless body.

An erratic ATC pulls alongside the medical aid boat and a River Rat yells that they have many casualties aboard. I instinctively jump into the boat in distress and see a well deck of blood and wounded soldiers lying in several masses, some sprawled on top of others. An enemy B-40 rocket has exploded inside the well deck. Of the twenty-nine in the platoon, two are dead and twenty-five are wounded. One has his guts exiting from a huge hole in his belly. Another is unconscious but still alive, with a large gaping hole where his left ear once was. Brain matter is oozing from the gap.

Burst cans of C rations litter the floor of the boat. A River Rat is lying on his back with a hole in his chest large enough to place a fist. Another soldier has much of his outer skin blown away. Most are soaked in sweat and blood. Some of the wounded are hysterical while others are unconscious.

Our three companies finally are able to beach, but the enemy is everywhere. Charlie Taylor says,

> I had a certain amount of fatalism when we went ashore after the two horrendous ambushes earlier in the day. I decided that today was as good a day as any other to buy the farm. Enemy fire was coming from many directions. I would have rather died in a set piece battle than by a sniper or a booby trap. My driving desire was that I do my absolute best with my decisions as my men were of critical importance, and we all did our best to keep one another alive. We were fighting for each other and not particularly for our country. Adrenaline was pumping through us by the quart, and I literally tingled to my fingers and toes. I went into a "slow motion" time frame and I was able to perceive everything very clearly.

Charlie positions his soldiers but they cannot move. Enemy fire impedes forward movement. An enemy machine gunner opens up on him and splatters him with mud from imploding bullets. Charlie calls in artillery to within twenty-five meters of his position, saving his platoon.

Today is Guy P. Moore's twenty-first birthday and his first major battle.

> Hundreds of enemy were on both sides of the stream. The boat I was in was hit by a rocket-propelled grenade, killing one navy River Rat and wounding several soldiers. I was terrified, as we all were, but none of us were willing to show the fear that was consuming us. Later in the battle, when it was time for my platoon to beach, the ramp on the boat dropped and we were running off firing our weapons into the thick jungle as we made our assault. We pushed forward until dark and then set our perimeter. A close friend named Dave Altman was with me and he said, "That's a hell of a party the VC gave you for your birthday. I hope the VC don't throw me a party like that on my birthday." We grinned in our fear. [Three weeks later, Dave was killed, never to see his birthday.]

After nightfall, fighting is sporadic. Tony Normand has his men positioned and Tony himself is half submerged on the bank of the river. During the night, he feels a slight tug on his leg; in the glow of the overhead flares he sees the tug is from the body of an enemy soldier killed upstream, floating gently in the slow-moving stream.

Between the army infantry and the navy River Rats, in the battle of Snoopy's Nose, we had 7 killed and 133 wounded.

Terry Gander says, "The volume of fire received and returned by us all day was deafening. This battle has been pressed in my memory for over forty years. It was truly a very traumatic experience for others and me as well. I will never forget it."

FEBRUARY 26–27, 1968

Over a battalion of enemy had been spotted near Can Tho and Company B 3/60th was quickly assembled to fly in and engage them. No artillery prep was fired into the enemy area in order to try and surprise them. This proved to be a huge mistake, as Company B was dropped right in the middle of the enemy. Fire was received immediately, and of the twelve choppers taking the troops, every one was hit except one. One chopper crashed and burned on-site.

Mitch Perdue says,

We landed in high grass and firing was coming from everywhere. We knew we had to run for cover, but we ran in the wrong direction—right toward the enemy. Soon, Keith May was hit in the stomach. Atkinson was killed during the night by our own gunships. Lt. Edwards was dead. I had only been in country a short time and this was absolutely the worst living nightmare I could imagine.

Squad leader Sgt. Plumer M. Barden Jr., who was also in that fight, said this about Mitch in that battle:

We went into an enemy stronghold that was horseshoe shaped, and as we flew in, our chopper was hit with intense fire. Mitch and the other soldiers jumped off when the chopper was about twenty-five feet off the ground, hitting the ground with a lot of force. Soon after landing, Mitch was hit in the upper right side of his mouth, knocking out one tooth and half of another one. He later got hit on the top of his left hand and still later was hit in his flak jacket in his left shoulder, causing a huge black-and-blue bruise. Although [he was] several times wounded, we couldn't get Mitch and many other wounded evacuated until the next day. We were pinned down for four to five hours before Echo Company came to our assistance. As they came to the enemy's right rear, we attacked the enemy positions and overran them, though this engagement caused us to have twelve killed and fifty-two wounded. Later that night, we would lose more in another part of the battle.

Guy P. Moore says,

As Bravo Company was landing, we had approximately 130 men. As we went in, we were hit immediately and later learned that we were completely surrounded by the enemy battalion. We lost about half of our men in the landing zone. We took a fierce pounding from rocket-propelled grenades, automatic weapons, and small-arms fire. The order was given to assault the tree line, because it was either stay where we were and all be killed or take the tree line and hope other units came in to help. I really believed that I was going to die that night. My stomach hurt so badly from the intense fear that gripped us all. In fact, I can still feel it when something bothers me.

As Bravo Company was up to their eyelids in VC fire, Echo Company was quickly called to fly in to help them. They were airlifted into the rice paddy next to where Company B was pinned down and taking massive casualties.

John Adame, with Echo Company, vividly remembers that afternoon and night as one of the worst he ever experienced.

As we flew in, a chopper ahead of us had crashed and was consumed with flames. We knew immediately that we were flying into the pits of hell. A canal separated us from Company B and we set our skirmish line at a right angle and I was about twenty yards from a banana grove. I was lying in a small canal. We were hit hard. My buddies pulled back, but I had the radio and felt it was my duty to stay. Suddenly, I realized I was all alone. I was absolutely scared shitless. I was alone for several hours as the battle raged all around me. During the night, I knew I must move into the nearby banana grove for better cover. As I crawled there, I heard someone say, "Don't fire. It must be an American because he is making too much noise for a VC." It was my buddies and they could have unknowingly killed me. Tracers were flying through the air in every direction.

I stayed put and near the end of the fight, I saw two VC firing into our banana grove and called in fire on them. During the night, several from Echo were killed, including my platoon sergeant. This was a very hard blow for me because I was very close to him.

Both companies set up along a canal around dusk and as nighttime came, all quieted down. We were to soon learn that the enemy had not left, but were regrouping. Around 1:00 a.m., all hell broke loose again. The VC en masse was trying to overrun our positions. It was pitch black and fire was going in all directions. Many VC were hit and we could hear them screaming. There was lots of yelling and crying. RPG rounds were landing all around us and tracers filled the dark night. Gunships came in firing mini guns and rockets into our perimeter trying to keep the gooks off of us. No doubt some of our people were killed by our gunships, but that was the only thing that kept the rest of us from being overrun and completely annihilated.

Guy P. Moore says,

In the morning, it was a little foggy and hazy, but thankfully the enemy had left. What was left of my company was stumbling around looking for anyone who was left alive. I hooked up with John Iannucci, Mike Barefield, and Don Sholty. Medevac choppers were coming in and we were helping to load the wounded and dead. When the headcount was taken, we had only one officer and one staff sergeant left and twenty-four enlisted, many of whom were walking wounded. The only officer left, Lt. Grayson Raulston, told us we were going to hold our heads high and walk out of there like men. He knew we all wanted to cry, but our tears have continued for four decades.

We lost so many friends during that fight and saw so many horrible things. I was never right in the head after that battle. I became a loner, and had no desire to make new friends or ever get close to anyone again. Losing good buddies is so hard to take. The God I once believed in as a boy died in Can Tho, and to this day I still have trouble getting close to God. . . .

My picture is on the cover of Jim Johnson's book, *Combat Chaplain*, and I can still remember what I was thinking when that photo was taken and we were standing in formation at that memorial service. I was saying to God, "Why, God, why did these kids have to die, and when will it be my turn?" I just wanted to go home so badly, but I knew I still had four months to go.

There would be nothing to ever compare with the trauma, hurt, intense fear, and deep pain that we all went through that day and night. As I sit here writing about Can Tho, my armpits are soaked. It's still very much with me.

John Iannucci was one of the soldiers who was hit but was a walking wounded. Lt. Cragin was hit near John. Later, Cragin was told that a chopper would soon be there to take him out. Cragin refused evacuation, insisting that others be evacuated first. Later that night, Cragin was hit again and killed. When the fight ended early the next morning, John was one of the 26 soldiers left of approximately 130 in Company B who went in. Twenty-two had been killed and over 80 were wounded severely enough to have to be evacuated after the battle ended. "All were brothers and some were very close friends," says John.

I was on the medical aid boat when the battle began. This is what I say in my book, *Combat Chaplain*:

I catch a ride to the Colleton. . . . Several doctors, nurses and medics have gathered awaiting the casualties. . . . The dustoffs make steady runs bringing soldiers whose flesh is torn and mutilated. . . . I am told that even the company commander, Captain Jim McDonald, has been shot. . . . One soldier has the back part of his head blown off and a navy doctor tells me he'll be blind for the rest of his life. . . . I reel with the thought that this nineteen-year-old kid will never again see a friend smile, pick out a beautiful flower for his girlfriend, or even look up a phone number. . . . I suddenly have a violent urge to let out a primal scream. . . . Keith May was shot in the stomach and was in the mud for nine hours before any of his buddies could get to him and get him out. Keith then demanded his buddies be dusted off before him, even though he was severely wounded. . . . Numerous body bags line the passageway next to the ship's bulkhead. . . . Hot tears begin to run down my cheeks. . . . I spoke with some of these guys on the pontoon this morning. . . . I cry for them and also for myself. Any of these lifeless forms in these body bags could have been me. . . . It's as if eight and one-half months of feelings are breaking loose. . . . These guys had no one to hold them as they drew their last breath. I now do the next best thing that comes to mind. I bend over each body bag and touch their heads, one by one, saying nothing. . . . I don't know if they're officer or enlisted, white, black or Hispanic, big or small. They're all dead. I love them so very much.

. . . . As the few surviving troops unload onto the pontoon, trauma shows on all their mud- and blood-covered young faces. . . . Some look like zombies, some still look terrified. . . . I soon learn that one soldier in John Iannucci's squad took fragment wounds early and refused to be evacuated only to be hit again later during the night and killed. . . . I feel void . . . lethargic. . . . I feel like my insides have been cut out! I don't ever recall feeling as empty and confused as I do now.

AUGUST 12–13, 1968

Having been sent out to relieve another unit, C/4/47th was walking on line across a rice paddy in a relatively "safe" area—or so it was thought. Then, all hell broke loose. Roy Moseman and Dave Schoenian were in the same platoon and remember the frightening details. Roy says,

We had walked into a battalion of VC. We were pinned down in the rice paddy for a couple of hours and then crawled back and took cover behind a dike. We kept fighting until after dark. Thinking all the enemy had left, around 2:00 a.m. one of my new men in my position said that he saw something in the paddy moving. I thought it was his imagination since he was a new replacement. I looked out and could not believe what I saw. VC were everywhere. We opened up on them with everything we had and called in artillery. The rounds were so close that a 155mm round exploded about ten feet behind us. Several of us received small pieces of shrapnel. The VC stormed right at our position. We were throwing hand grenades at them and they were throwing them at us. Some of the VC got within twenty feet of us before we killed them. Then we ran out of ammunition. I ordered my men to crawl back to the rest of the platoon. Then I threw my last grenade and crawled back myself. By daylight the fight was over and the paddy lay full of dead VC.

Dave Schoenian says of that battle,

As we were being overrun that night, one position of guys who were hit first were screaming as they were being brutally killed. The artillery was dropping short rounds and the last one landed right behind us in the mud. We were near to hand-to-hand fighting. I saw a gook throw a hand grenade at me just as I shot him, but the grenade landed on the other side of the dike I was lying behind.

Dave and Roy's platoon had seven brothers killed that night, and the company had a total of fifteen killed.

Excerpts, yes. In addition to these three battles, we could write for days about more battles. But these are only a *very few* of hundreds of other snippets of combat trauma that we sixteen have lived with for these four decades. The rest of our writings center on the effects of our tragedy, trauma, and memories of these horrible events.

4

BROKEN BODIES, MINDS, AND BROTHERHOOD

To be wounded in combat leaves scars that are forever reminders of the high price some of us pay in serving our country. It also reminds us that we came so very close to death when the shell fragment or bullet hit us. In our first firefight, our souls are impregnated with the reality that combat is very deadly, and for a very young person to be thrust into this state is to mark him for the rest of his life. Combat savagely impacts us physically, spiritually, emotionally, and relationally. We daily faced death in an environment unlike any of our short lives had ever experienced or imagined. We quickly bonded with our combat brothers, who were in the same chaotic and dangerous situation.

The good news is that wounds to our bodies heal. The bad news is that the emotional effects of our combat trauma are with us for a lifetime. All of us have inner conflicts in the deepest recesses of our minds resulting from the loss of brothers, and sometimes it feels like we are losing or have lost our minds. Losing brothers to death or evacuation when we never see that person again is described by Tony Normand as "secrets of the brotherhood that no Saigon desk jockey or most Americans can or will ever comprehend."

In the States, when a tragedy occurs such as a school bus wreck, a police shooting, a school massacre, or a natural disaster, grief counselors are brought in, families offer an ear and support, our churches pray with and for us, and the community at large shares in what one has just experienced. The abnormality of young combat troops was that we had no way to be nurtured by those who loved us the most. As youngsters, we often needed to be with loved ones. We couldn't even make a phone call to our mother or have someone to sob with. We never had a chance to talk to a grief counselor or get psychological counseling, or have time to grieve or in any way time to make sense out of what had just happened. When a firefight ended, it was always, "Evacuate the wounded and dead and get ready to move out." We always had another combat operation that took precedence over "sissy" things like needing to mourn our dead and get our own heads together.

Seeing so much violence at times was overpowering, and many times all of us would go close to "the edge." Mentally, none of us ever knew how much we could take. Dave Schoenian says, "Learning to kill is easy. Learning not to kill is the hard part. You become uncontrollable and take your revenge out on anything. I got so upset one day, I shot a water buffalo eighteen times and burned down several uninhabited hooches."

Being on death row is how Guy P. Moore felt as a combat infantry soldier.

We would go out on an operation for a few days, and most of the time lived in hell. Then we would rest up, clean our weapons, and attend a memorial service for our dead friends. Then it was time to go back into the jungle, and do it all over again until you went home, either on the freedom bird or in a body bag. Knowing this and seeing many of your brothers leave like this was a ton of trauma for a young man just out of his teen years. No wonder we combat veterans have had such a hard time dealing with everyday life.

We became brothers immediately when a new troop arrived, and in each firefight, we were fighting for each other. In many cases, very heroic deeds were done in trying to protect one another. It is a terrible reality that once a brother in our squad is hit, we evacuate him and, in many cases, once the medevacchopper flies over the tree line on the way to the hospital, we never see or hear from him again. This loss can leave holes in our souls, for a brother is gone! Combat violence extracts a brother from our lives like a vampire savagely cutting out our heart. The aftermath of our combat trauma not only mangled us but impacts succeeding generations as well.

Imagine what would have happened after the Virginia Tech rampage in 2007 had the school leaders simply required the surviving students to remove the wounded and dead, clean up the blood and gore, and then an hour later declare the event over, telling everyone to return to class as if nothing has happened. Imagine then that the next day there was another shooting on campus. Again, the gore was cleaned up and students were told to return to class as if nothing had happened. Play this scene over dozens of times. Ludicrous? Absolutely! Yet, that's exactly what happened to us. It is no wonder that our unmourned grief often turned to rage, depression, and withdrawal, and nightmares haunted us for the rest of our lives. Many of us felt betrayed and exploited, which resulted in paranoia, meaninglessness, despair, drug and alcohol use, and even suicide.

Leaving a firefight and heading to the river to be extracted in May 1967, Terry Gander, Charlie Fleming, and Fincher were pulling rear security until the platoon had boarded the extraction boats. When this threesome was heading to the boat, they were hit by small-arms and automatic weapons fire, with Fincher being hit in the leg. Returning fire, Fleming carried Fincher piggyback and Terry carried Fleming's and Fincher's field gear and weapons. "Once we evacuated Fincher, I never saw or heard from him again."

In a nipa palm grove on November 21, 1967, Terry heard the snap of a booby trap grenade, heard the explosion, and then saw the smoke. Carl Moser, a very good friend, was hit, as was Terry. Terry chose not to be evacuated since his shrapnel wound was small, but Carl was evacuated—and, again, Terry never saw his good buddy again.

After losing so many good brothers, it became painful to get close to other new guys because, as John Adame says, "Everyone seemed to get killed that I got close to." Dave Altman, a very good buddy of Guy P. Moore, was killed in a hot landing zone on October 6, 1967. Guy says, "It has been forty years since my friend died out in that open rice paddy, but I can still see his smile and hear his voice."

When not on operations, we stayed on board the navy barracks ships in the Mekong River and its tributaries. When we finished an operation, we would return to rest, clean up, and get some hot food prior to returning on the next operation. Living in the tight quarters on board, many of us were in very compact areas of ship bunks, with a dozen or so brothers sleeping in very close proximity. Vacancies in bunks always occurred after a fire-fight when brothers were killed or evacuated. Mitch Perdue says that after that terrible battle on February 26–27, 1968, "when I returned back to the ship, the empty beds of so many dead brothers was almost more than I could take." Mitch, John Iannucci, Guy P. Moore, and others who had survived had the daunting task of packing up the personal belongings of their dead brothers. To say this was difficult is a glaring understatement.

After leaving Vietnam, and after many years, some of us have been successful in re-establishing contact with some of our brothers. More about that later in our writings. However, some of the brothers were so broken as a result of their combat trauma that they want nothing to do with any remembrances of their trauma, including their brothers. Erol Tuzcu phoned a Vietnam brother a few years ago and he refused to talk. John Iannucci had a very good friend who, though he talked to John, was so wounded in his soul that he denied to his immediate family that he had even been to Vietnam, much less to let them know of his trauma. Charlie Taylor was very good friends with a fellow platoon leader who was severely wounded and evacuated. This lieutenant was a happy and jovial officer and was respected. A few years ago, Charlie located him and phoned him. Their brief conversation went like this: "This is Charlie Taylor from Vietnam." "Charlie, Vietnam was a part of my life that is in the past. Goodbye." Click.

"To face your mortality at such a young age, to see your friends slaughtered, coming back to the unit without some guys was so terrible and has left a hole in my soul to this day," is how Bob Stumpf sees it. An ambush on April 7, 1968, killed Joseph Rees, Jan (Bobo) Bobowski, Brown, Tate, and Erickson, all in Bob's platoon. Joe Rees and Bob were very close friends, having been through Basic and AIT together.

> At the last reunion of the Mobile Riverine Force Association, Joe's brother, Jerry Rees, along with his wife and daughter, attended our memorial service that was officiated by our chaplain, Jim Johnson. While draining, to be reconnected to Joe's family after forty years was unique, to say the least.

Most of us did not have close relationships with the Vietnamese. However, Ray Shurling and his fellow Special Forces soldiers found a small Vietnamese boy wandering in the jungle. His parents had been killed by the VC and the child had no other family. Ray and his brothers "adopted" the boy and they took care of him in their base camp. They called him Paco. They grew very close. When the day came for Ray to leave for the states, it was like leaving his son, never to be seen again. "Our eyes met. I was so very excited at going home but oh, so sad, to leave Paco behind. My heart still aches for this child. I can still see his face and wonder if he survived."

Ray had also become very close to Boyd Newbold during their Special Forces training. Boyd was on leave in Utah and Ray left for Vietnam two days early in order to stop in Utah so these two best buddies could leave together. "Boyd's sister Nancy did not go to the airport with us. She did not say good-bye. Instead, it was 'See you later.' She felt that would help him get home safely." The last thing Ray said to Boyd's family was a promise that he'd see that Boyd was OK. Of course, that was a promise that Ray could not keep, regardless of intent. Boyd was killed soon after arriving in Vietnam.

Over the years, Ray says,

> I wanted to make contact with Boyd's family. But I could not gather the courage to make the call. For years I had the number. Many times I would get drunk, hold the phone and the number in front of me, but I just couldn't dial the number. I would often break down and cry. Once I broke the handset of a phone on the kitchen table because I did not have, nor could I gather the courage to make the call. I have lived with this pain for thirty-eight years.

It was not until 2007 that Ray decided to locate Boyd's family. Since then, Ray has been in contact with both a brother and two sisters of Boyd and is making plans to travel to Utah later for a visit.

A different twist for Ray, though, occurred with his father. Ray's parents divorced when he was ten. His father was career army and in the following ten years, Ray seldom saw his father as he was stationed in Germany, France, Thailand, and Alaska. While Ray was stationed in Vietnam, his father was also stationed there with an engineer unit building a bridge.

Good things can happen even in Vietnam. During our two visits there, my dad and I reconnected as father-son. I was twenty-one. We talked man to man and sorta cleared the air. I got things off my chest. He was rather proud to introduce his son wearing that green beret. From this day forward we were very close until the day he died.

I had become close with a Vietnamese pastor in My Tho, but the Tet offensive scattered Pastor Ha and his family, and I left Vietnam never knowing what became of them. It was not until 1996, when John Iannucci and I returned to Vietnam, that I was to learn what had happened to them. Happily, they all survived the war.

And, so, for the most part, we were broken—in body, mind, and brotherhood. We had been dependent on every other brother we fought with, and now we are disintegrated as a brotherhood. Wasn't it enough to have lost dear friends? Wasn't the terror, horror, and shock of combat enough? We were a brotherhood of soldiers who needed each other. Some of our dear brothers were individuals with whom, in the safety of the States, we might have never become friendly, much less close friends. In Vietnam, we fought for them, but had no chance to mourn their deaths. We had to throw their bodies aboard a chopper without ceremony, often under fire. Then, our dead were actually handled by total strangers. We couldn't even attend a wake, or grieve with their families or with our surviving brothers. When a brother was hit, he was removed, and we prepared to "move out" on another operational objective. We had no chance to process what had just happened.

We were young kids who became old men after the first firefight. Sometimes, we even wonder if it all happened that way, or if it happened at all. Some of our personalities were wrecked and we still have grossly unhealed emotional combat wounds four decades later. We still need to mourn because, back then, tears were dangerous and grief was fragmented, deflected, disregarded, dreaded, and even mocked by our leaders who had not been there. Beyond our company commanders, our superior officers did not taste the hazards of close combat and couldn't understand.

Much of life is massacred as a result of the violence of combat, which has sent deep roots into our hearts. It has no seasons and always seems ripe. When it is over, we often ask if the sacrifices were worth the "causes." When life is mangled, where does the previous meaning of life go? Yes, at times we were emotionally spent and we collapsed, either there or after we returned to the States. In order to survive, we often had no choice but to just stop feeling . . . any kind of feelings. Even compassion often vacated our souls. Our depersonalization as young kids never allowed us to get used to the insanity of combat. In order to tolerate the destruction all around, we often developed the mantra "It don't mean shit" as a means to just get by emotionally.

If someone had thirty or forty experiences like Columbine or Virginia Tech, could any young person survive emotionally? What are the emotional consequences of having to kill and destroy? Our state of shock still comes and goes. In some ways, we are stuck between being now older men and frightened and disintegrated youngsters in combat.

And so, we returned after our tours as damaged goods. Our government just wanted us to go away. It was like the effects of combat trauma were just an illusion. Few Americans who have not been in combat have ever even touched a dead body, much less put a buddy in a body bag and made sure you got all the body parts stuffed in properly. All of us as young soldiers saw more dead and mangled bodies from combat than the average American would see in a thousand years.

Coming back to the States, some of us were labeled as malingerers and having had personality disorders since childhood. The denial of our government tethered with the lack of understanding of those to whom we returned has made us all realize that there are no flak jackets or steel helmets for the soul and mind. Many of us are still numbed out, feel tainted, and even have difficulty enjoying the simplest of pleasures.

Our combat trauma was like being burned on the inside, and each time we were burned emotionally, instead of being toughened, we became more and more vulnerable and fragmented. How we wish our trauma was like a splinter that could be extracted with simple tweezers or a painful tooth that could be filled or extracted. No, it is with us for the duration of our lives. Certainly, we are very gratified that we had ways to evacuate our wounded to the finest surgeons and medical care possible in a combat zone. But there has been no way to evacuate our wounded souls.

After four decades, our combat violence still grabs us by the scruff of the neck and jerks us around. We still find ourselves wondering how we are supposed to behave after having beaten and brutalized others and having been beaten and brutalized ourselves. Our minds often are like a rubber band about to snap due to our flashbacks, triggers, and nightmares of the trauma of combat.

It is often heard, "I know a Vietnam combat veteran, and boy, is he messed up." What they see often is an exhausted spirit and the infamous thousand-yard stare, which is when we are caught up in the moment and are entranced by events four decades ago of standing over dead bodies, looking to kill more before we become a dead body ourselves. How were we supposed to feel and act after standing over those mangled bodies we had just watched getting blown away? Our emotions were stretched very tight and often our souls stayed exhausted. Soon, we just had to "stop feeling." Adopting that "It don't mean shit" slogan served as a means to keep our fragile psyches lightly glued together.

Yes, our broken bodies healed. But our broken minds and brotherhood remain constant sources of pain. And, we returned home . . .

II

HOME (BITTER) SWEET HOME

We were not sure what to expect when we returned, but for sure we wanted home to be like we left it when we left that "place" ten thousand miles from home. For those of us who were not medically evacuated, the much-anticipated trip home was to be via "freedom bird," appropriately depicting the complex fact that we had been incarcerated for our tour. We would return to "the world," indicating that we had been in outer space.

From the day of arrival in Vietnam, many of us began to count the days until our year was completed so we could return home. Some of us even made "short-timers" calendars so we could mark off each day. Thoughts of returning home were indeed sweet. However, as we were soon to learn, there were more than sufficient "bitter pills" that were awaiting us on our return home.

5

ON THE HOME FRONT

Likewise, it was not our desire for our homecoming to be seen as our "whining," but rather as the reality of it being significantly less than we deserved. We thought we could leave Vietnam and it would all be behind us but we were soon to learn that we couldn't leave any of it behind.

(UN)WELCOME HOME

When we left Vietnam, we returned with no debriefing about how we should feel or act. However, most of us were told to take our uniform off as soon as possible because the antiwar hippies might meet us at the airports and it would be unpleasant. "Expect protesters at the airport; they may throw water balloons or rotten fruit at you and the balloons may be filled with piss. There may be derogatory signs. You may be spit upon. But you can't retaliate. You can be charged if you do." How can the military and civilian authorities allow this? Why are *we* the target of their anger? If we had been in a bad wreck, would it have been acceptable to be treated like this when the ambulance unloaded us at the hospital? We are still dumbfounded at the irony of this.

I had my wife, two little children, and my parents to come home to. Initially, I just wanted to rest. After a couple of days, Barbara and I decided to visit some friends. They in turn invited some other friends over as well. "What was it like in Vietnam?" I was asked. What was I to say? "There was death and destruction everywhere we went"? However, before I could even answer, the subject immediately shifted to next year's football season. "Who in hell wants to talk about football, when I just returned from so much trauma," I thought. Even though I had been an all-state football player, football seemed so very trivial now.

More friends were visited and the question again came up about Vietnam. When I mentioned about how many of my soldiers had been killed, they immediately shifted the conversation to Buddhist monks torching themselves and the political climate in Vietnam. "Who cares about that? What about what *I've* just experienced?" were the unanswered questions burning in my soul. The lesson was being branded into me that no one really wants to know about any details of buddies with blown-off legs, blinded eyes, bowels exiting from gaping holes in their bellies. and brains oozing from head wounds. To tell it like it really was risked emptying the room, figurative and literally. So, for several decades, I and many of us just shut up and tried to bury our massacred memories deep inside.

John Iannucci's day of departure from Vietnam was like a roller coaster. He was overjoyed but felt guilty that he was leaving his buddies and that he had survived and many had not. As the plane took off, the cheers of the GIs were deafening, but they quickly died down as each troop retreated in hours of reflection of their tour. When they landed in California, John and three other GIs had a four-hour layover. They went to a local bar for a beer and were asked, "How old are you boys?" They had been in hell for a year and had experienced in that year what a thousand civilians would not experience in a lifetime. Yet they were too young to order a beer. John later arrived at LaGuardia in New York in uniform, and four cabbies declined to give him a ride home to Staten Island because there was no guarantee of a return fare.

When John arrived home, his father had planned a welcome-home party the next day. John felt uneasy. There were plenty of "How are you" and "Glad to see you" comments. But no one went any further. These were only perfunctory comments by well-intentioned friends and family. John felt very out of place as he could not relate to what they were involved with, all of which seemed so trivial in view of what he had just left.

During the party John's father and two of his WWII buddies were talking and he walked up to them. They were telling *their* WWII stories. However, not once did any of them bring up anything about John's experiences. Maybe they didn't know what to ask. Maybe they wanted to protect John from having to think or talk about unpleasant things. Yet "I was bursting inside just wanting to let someone know what was really happening in Vietnam and what had happened to me." This type of patronizing attitude led us to take an important first step: Don't talk, for there is no one who can hear or who wants to hear.

Guy P. Moore's life of post-Vietnam rebellion began immediately, as he learned that American society was treating him like an outcast. He quickly turned into a confused, hurt, and often violent young man whom people did not want to be around. Guy actually got into a fight at a bar within hours after arriving in California from Vietnam and spent the night in jail. This was the first of numerous fights in the future that caused much difficulty for a very troubled young veteran. He had been in "combat mode" for months and remained in that mode for years.

Ron Miriello attended a dinner party with his father a few days after his arrival home. Immediately, Ron realized he was very anxious and had some ease only if he faced the door, sat in the corner, and had a "line of sight."

Flying into Buffalo, New York, Bob Nichols was met at the airport by his parents for a joyous welcome. After a two-hour drive home, Bob's brother met them at the front door with the devastating news that "Grandpa" had just died an hour before. This was the man who had taught Bob about hard work, perseverance, and honesty. Bob learned carpentry and masonry work from him. He was the last person Bob saw in his hometown when he left for Vietnam. "This was a hell of a thing to come home to after just going through so much combat. I was again devastated."

Roy Moseman states,

No one understood me. Friends and family didn't know what was inside me. I didn't know how to explain it to them. Then, after a while, I didn't want to. I went out every night and got drunk so that I could sleep. At times I felt very lonely because I had all these problems going on but did

not feel comfortable talking seriously about them to anyone. It felt like I
was the only one in the world having the nightmares and depression.

Bob Stumpf took a taxi home during a snowstorm. The cabbie tried
to rip him off with the fare by charging three times the fare to take him
from JFK airport to the Bronx. Infuriated, Bob told him to f--- himself
and threw him a ten-dollar bill.

After Bob arrived at the Bronx on leave, he was in total shock. As he
walked around the neighborhood, it felt like people were staring at him.
He felt like a displaced refugee. He did not belong anymore. He felt out
of place even in a bar. At twenty-one, he felt like an old man. It felt like
"the whole world was in a shitter. People do die when you shoot them. I
could have been killed numerous times. But, who cares now? Who can
listen?" Bob's shock led to an emotional shutdown.

John Adame, being proud to be home, told the cab driver from the
airport, "I'm just back from Vietnam." "Big f------ deal, how many babies
did you kill?" responded the crass cabbie. That cabbie never knew how
close he came to having John savagely beat his head in. Two days later,
John, his brother, and a friend of his brother were in his backyard. His
brother told the friend that John had just returned from Vietnam and
said didn't he want to speak to him. John was sitting under a tree a few
feet away. The friend refused. Later it was learned that the friend was
frightened because John "looked like he wanted to kill someone."

Dave Schoenian returned and "got wild." He spent three months running crazy. His family was frightened of him.

Ray Shurling returned with much pride, but that soon was squashed.

At twenty-one, I felt just as much a patriot as those at Fort McHenry when
the "Star-Spangled Banner" was written. But we were forgotten by friends,
misunderstood by family, and scorned by the media. There were no patriotic
songs, no bands, and no parades. We got nothing—not even a thank-you. We
veterans did not turn our backs on America or the star-spangled banner. We
held Old Glory high in our hearts while the hippies burned her in the streets.
Yet I would take up the banner again today and defend her if called.

On leave at home attending a wedding reception with lots of alcohol
available, Ray was engaged in a conversation with a Coast Guard veteran
who spent WWII "protecting Savannah, Georgia, from the Germans."

In our discussion, I told him if I had a son old enough to go to Vietnam, I'd do all I could to keep him out of there. That arrogant son-of-a-bitch who never heard a shot fired in battle called me a coward and traitor, and I immediately hit him in the mouth as hard as I could. He hit the wall and fell to the floor. Friends grabbed me and pulled me away as I tried to get to him again. We fell to the floor and my head hit a table and I was nearly knocked out. After I was dragged outside, a friend asked, "What the f--- is wrong with you, man? Have you gone crazy?"

After being discharged, at the insistence of his mother, Ray joined the VFW to "get involved and do good deeds. I did not fit in at all. The final straw was when a WWII vet told me, 'You boys didn't fight no real war. Vietnam is a police action.' I never went to another meeting."

The only thank-you that Ray received was when he went to his family physician, Dr. Johnnie Gallamore, for a checkup shortly after discharge. When Ray was ready to write his check, Dr. Gallamore said simply, "No charge. Thank you for doing your duty." This remembrance still brings tears to Ray's eyes today.

Erol Tuzcu, the Turkish immigrant who was drafted into the U.S. Army when he could hardly speak English, was treated "like Vietnam was all our fault and our idea."

Bob Nichols was very sociable prior to going to Vietnam. He liked to stand out. However, after returning from combat, he wanted to stay in the background. His attitude had changed. It didn't help that more than one antagonist called him a "f------ cold-blooded killer." Those antagonists were lucky they didn't become victims.

So, most of us were really alone. It was like each of us were two different persons; one was what our family and friends remembered us as being and what they wanted us to be, and the other was having morbid and heart-wrenching stories in our hearts that needed to be told and heard. Unfortunately, we had to go it alone because we quickly learned that whoever heard our stories would be torn, shaken, and speechless. Our unhealed combat trauma left many of us with no tongue to tell our stories and no trust that anyone would hear and understand without judgment if we did tell. So we shut up—and took our pain inside. Psychologically and relationally, many of us are trapped in a time warp somewhere over the Pacific, no longer in Vietnam but not home either, for home was not like it was when we left.

We were mystified at being accused of being baby killers, of committing torture and atrocities; at the media image of us being crazy, drug addicted, and violent; and, for all practical purposes, at not being understood or cared for by our community. In fact, we are still mystified and still being lied about by politicians who have used us to win votes.

We came home feeling like we had been lost and trapped in a dark cave for many months and didn't see the light of day for all that time. Then, when we finally emerged from the cave, we were spit upon at the entrance of the cave, shunned, and marginalized by those near and far. Certainly, there could be no celebration when there was so much contempt.

There are times when someone will ask, "Why aren't you over Vietnam? That's been four decades." Sometimes, this question and implied judgment results in expressions of rage. It reinforces that we came home alone, not unlike walking point alone, not knowing what to expect or when we are going to be ambushed.

Welcome home? It feels to most of us that this statement can be understood only by other combat veterans. *Welcome home!*

WE'RE HOME: IS SOMETHING WRONG?

It did not take us long to realize that what we left at home was not the same now. Much of "it" seemed to have changed, when in fact the "it" was us. While at times it was difficult to pin down exactly what was troubling so many of us, there was no doubt that things had happened to us that had transformed our lives in some rather unorthodox ways. Combat had set us apart from the norm of American society. Many of us had taken risks of dying for something that few, including us, even understood.

America at large expected us to return from combat like returning from an out-of-town high school sporting event and to pick up life like our trauma never occurred. No one seemed to care that while our peers at home were going to fraternity parties, fishing, hunting, dating, and otherwise living the "good life," we were performing tasks of killing, maiming, and destroying while just trying to stay alive for one more day.

Most of us immediately felt all alone, yet none of us deserved to have to sort through our combat trauma alone. No doubt, the inability to talk about our combat trauma has given us cause for untold pain for decades since. Not only had we not been welcomed home, we often felt compelled to keep silent and, in some cases, even to deny we had even served in Vietnam.

Our dammed-up combat trauma fast became an unhealthy cesspool. We did not want our lives to be so infected, yet our souls seemed so hollow. Little made sense anymore. Sometimes we would explode, attack, or strike out, and we often projected an empty and cold facade. It became difficult to find purpose or meaning in life. Oh, we so badly wanted things at home to be like they were before. But our insides felt they had been reamed out, and there was little there but our seared soul. We became very guarded and careful not to let others see the torment hidden just below the surface.

We feared that even if we could talk about it, we might be seen as weak or somehow unable to deal with it. Sometimes our thoughts were, "If you had experienced what I experienced, it'd screw you up, too." Many of us hid our feelings with excessive drinking, withdrawal, and blunting our feelings. Few of us were willing to risk being transparent to others by revealing our deep emotional wounds that often were just below the surface. The one exception was anger. Often unwarranted and unexpected rage or a burst of anger seemed to come out of nowhere, often unfairly directed at those who loved us the most: our spouses and children. Other times, our anger surfaced in the form of cynicism. This often confused those who loved us and added to the mystery of how different we had become.

We lived with the dreams/nightmares, feelings of being back in Vietnam, survival guilt, suppression, sleep difficulties, uneasiness in crowds, memories of the blood, guts, torn limbs, agony, and all-night screams of wounded buddies—and smells. We lived with the memories of physical depletion, immersion foot, despair, death from the enemy and sometimes from friendly fire, and the pounding heart from remembering the first shot in an ambush. We were stimulated by the memory of smells of blood and death. We couldn't retreat then, but now we can—or so we think.

Sometimes we cried, but almost always in private. There were times when we feared that if we weren't careful, our crying would cause us to get completely out of control, and if that occurred, we very well might lose our mind and be put away.

We didn't want to be associated with the growing number of vets who slept under bridges, were suicidal, and in general were misfits. Yet many of us drank excessively, had trouble with relationships, had trouble at work, and became very good at denying to ourselves that something could possibly be wrong with us.

Time did not heal our emotional wounds. It seemed that they always seemed to surface at inopportune times. Combat violence had sent deep roots into our hearts and souls; it had no seasons; it always seemed ripe.

Deciding to stay in the army, I moved my family to Fort Bliss, Texas, and worked as the stockade chaplain for the next two years. I was recognized in many ways as doing an outstanding job. However, I began to have troubling dreams and nightmares, flashbacks, and periods of sadness. Puzzled, I marveled for months that, even though many of the soldiers there had been to Vietnam, none seemed bothered by their experiences there. It took some time before I realized that Fort Bliss is an air defense post and the vets there were in Vietnam primarily as air defense soldiers. They spent their tour mostly inside a compound and had, at most, an occasional mortar attack—which is certainly frightening, but they certainly did not experience the daily combat trauma as did my infantry grunts.

As a chaplain, I saw my role as being a helper and healer to my soldiers who had personal problems. I developed a dichotomy that would last a lifetime: on the one hand I was the healer and on the other hand I was the wounded. A book written years later by Henri Nouwen was entitled *The Wounded Healer*—an apt description of my condition.

Bob Nichols knew immediately after arriving home that things were different.

> My family and friends were happy to see me, but I was extremely jumpy, edgy, kept my back against the wall in public places, found myself always checking who was coming in the door, et cetera. I had a couple of personal relationships that didn't work. At first I thought, "What in hell is wrong with those girls?" Guess what I learned? It wasn't them at all, it was me—but I couldn't explain it to myself even. . . .
>
> Prior to the war, I was an avid hunter. When I returned home, I bought my deer license, took my shotgun, and headed to the woods. I was walking across a hayfield with a wood line a couple hundred yards away. I suddenly stopped. I stared at the wood line, looked down at the shotgun in

my hands, stood there a few moments, then turned around and went back to the car and home. I have never been hunting again.

The war was still an everyday story. For John Iannucci, no one around him ever mentioned it. Even John didn't mention it. Yet, it consumed his daily thoughts. John bought into a small trucking business and buried himself in work with fourteen-hour days. Vietnam would pop into his mind with thoughts of terrible battles, horrific injuries, and helicopters burning. He even began to question whether these events really happened. "Was it true? Or did I just dream up these things. Why does no one care or even know about what happened? Why can't we talk about it?" John went deep inside of himself for most of the 1970s, and that decade for him is still a blur. In trying to understand and cope, John bought every book that came out on the Vietnam War.

Before Vietnam, Roy Moseman was an easygoing, fun-loving person with lots of emotion. After Vietnam, it was like no one understood him. Even his best friends and family didn't know what he had experienced in Vietnam nor what he was feeling inside, and he was unable to explain it to them. Roy came to believe that he was the only one who was feeling the sadness, depression, and nightmares. It was a very lonely feeling, not having anyone else to talk to or to really know what he was going through. His unhealed combat trauma left him almost like a mute. Like the rest of us, there still is not a day that goes by without thinking about Vietnam.

Roy entered the University of Georgia but dropped out during his junior year because of the disconnect of many of his professors with the real world. They seemed to live in a theoretical world, and Roy, the student, had seen and experienced more about life than the entire faculty would ever experience on their sterile and insulated campus.

Like most of the rest of us, Mitch Perdue fought his feelings alone. He didn't or couldn't talk about it because there was no one to hear his feelings, which were left in his gut to simmer for years to come.

Dave Schoenian went home to West Virginia and "went wild"—bars every night, worked a week, got laid off, took unemployment for a year and loafed with a buddy, went to coal mine training, stayed a week and quit, and finally his uncle took him to the power company. Like Bob Nichols, he then worked for the following thirty-three years for the power company.

Returning to the Bronx with a terrible hole in his soul, Bob Stumpf pretty much shut down and felt in shock during his earlier years after returning home. He felt emotionally crippled and stone-cold inside.

Difficulty focusing, concentrating, and remembering details greatly troubled Guy P. Moore. His anxiety increased tremendously when he was unable to focus while working on a project. This led to a degradation of his sense of self-esteem and self-worth.

Terry Gander also knew something was wrong with him, but, like most of us, thought he could handle it himself. Plus, he didn't want to be seen as "just another vet with problems." "It" eventually ate him up, and clinical depression and a mental breakdown finally got him to admit that what was wrong needed help from professionals in the hospital.

Charlie Taylor turned to his family of faith and his wife for support. Even though they did not know the details of Charlie's trauma, they loved him unconditionally.

Homecoming was another traumatic event for Erol Tuzcu. Like the rest of us, there was no debriefing; he was called names and experienced a hostile environment. He knew he had a monkey on his back, but it would be 1999 before he knew it had a name: PTSD. In the meantime, for years he just tried to "suck it up and be a man," whatever that means.

To help quell the pain and distressful memories, many of us turned to chemicals, alcohol, danger seeking, workaholism, and outrageous sex. Common comments from us today include: "I drank continuously and didn't know why." "I used to drink myself to sleep." "I consistently voiced feelings of hopelessness and of life having no purpose. I was very self-destructive and self-harming."

Even though we frequently saw ourselves as having something wrong with us, it also would infuriate us when someone else had the audacity to suggest that we were somehow different. "Why aren't you over the Vietnam stuff?" "Just forget it and move on." Sure, all of us would like to forget. Many of us tried for years to forget. But how do you forget? Would we want to forget the loss of a parent or a sibling? Certainly not. Deep down, we don't want to forget Vietnam, for to forget would mean a devaluation of the lives of our buddies whose lives were mangled physically or emotionally and the lives of those who died there.

Yes, something was wrong, but we weren't sure what.

6

IGNORED BY THE GOVERNMENT, SOCIETY, AND THE PUBLIC

President John F. Kennedy, in his inaugural address, made a comment to Americans: "Ask not what your country can do for you—ask what you can do for your country." These were moving and powerful words.

As young Americans fresh out of high school, our country asked (ordered) from us a task of enormous proportions: to go into combat. Even though we were ordered to do so, we had loyalty and believed in duty, honor, and country. We could have run, gone to prison, hidden, or gone to college for deferments. But we didn't. We went, as our nation ordered, in simple obedience to our duty as young citizens.

Reality was, however, that combat veterans were abandoned in several ways. First, we were abandoned on the battlefield. Our national leaders decided to fight this war by "out–body counting" the enemy. We became expendable! Individual life was seen as having no value. We were only a number. We killed because we were ordered as citizens to do so. Tactically, we fought the same battles in the same locations over and over again. Gaining ground was meaningless. Strategically, we were placed under severe limits as to where we could fight, and we were hogtied in our efforts. In the meantime, the killing fields were getting bloodier and bloodier.

It is no fun being expendable. In retrospect, our lives were useless and unimportant, as the body counts were the only thing that counted. Combat troops became no more than marbles on a playground or pawns on a chessboard. Our government lost all perspective of national objectives, however noble they were at the beginning. Yet our lives were being sacrificed daily while our government leaders floundered. We were expendable for no apparent reason other than a governmental logjam.

The people running the war had absolutely no concept of what it was like in the midst of an ambush. We combat soldiers were being robbed of our youth, health, sanity, and life itself while our leaders in Washington discussed whether bombs dropped on the Ho Chi Minh trail should be five hundred or a thousand pounds or whether the Paris peace table should be round, oblong, square, or whatever. If our leaders had had any understanding of the horror and terror that we were experiencing daily or if their lives were on point of our patrols, negotiations would have been around the clock for a settlement.

For the most part, supplies of ammunition, food, and necessities were very good. Nevertheless, early on in the war, basic items designed for the infantryman failed to reach us. Jungle hats were meant for grunts to wear on ambush sites to reduce the chances of noise revealing our positions to the enemy. Support troops in the major base camps had them, but it was months before the infantry received them. It also took months before we received tablets to heat C rations, and in the meantime, we had to burn a pinch of C-4 explosives to heat our food. Major base camps had a continual flow of USO shows, but it was not until later in the war that infantrymen were given the chance of attending them, and then it was via a lottery.

Second, many heartless individuals and groups treated combat veterans like it was all our fault. Certainly, there were the hated and self-centered egomaniacs from Hollywood who encouraged the opposing forces to kill American soldiers by visiting Hanoi and celebrating their status as stars when in reality many of them were the Benedict Arnolds to combat veterans. When we returned from a tour in combat, what right did anyone have to blame us for the war and to spit on us and call us names, and what right did the media have to write and report only of atrocities and torture and puke on us in the press? Sure, to protest the war and have antiwar beliefs were certainly their right. But to blame the veteran for it was lunacy at best and destructive at worst to those of us who had responded to our nation's call.

Hell's bells, it wasn't us who started the war! It wasn't us who wanted to kill! It wasn't us who wanted to see our brothers slaughtered! It wasn't us who made any of the decisions about how the war was run! All we did was to try and stay alive and keep our brothers alive and to return home to mom, apple pie, and life! But, to be vilified? Spit upon? Rejected? Blamed? Scapegoated? If we sound angry, yes, we are—even four decades later.

Third, the country at large had betrayed us. Few know of the terrible suffering we went through and the suffering from the effects of trauma we still experience. The average American sees combat only through the filtered eyes of history writers and films that portray the glory of Rambo or at best intellectualize it. This is pure insanity and denial. Combat is hell, and so few Americans seem to know or care.

Fourth, we were sent to war by our nation, who then turned against us. We were abandoned by our nation when we came home; they just wanted us to shut up, go away, and hide.

History tells us that we were not the first veterans who were rejected by our nation. After the Civil War, veterans roamed rural America looking for work, many with still unhealed wounds. They carried their hoes on their shoulders, willing to work for food. As a result, the nation began denigrating them by calling them hobos ("hoe boys"). In 1924 the government legislated bonuses for World War I vets, but they were not paid. When the vets marched on Washington, they were met with tanks and bayonets driven out of Washington, and their camps were burned.

When we returned, we were vilified for years. The Veterans Administration (VA) was an adversarial system. Side issues were treated, but continuing emotional problems of combat trauma were totally ignored. When we came home, the VA just didn't get it. It was "us versus them." We had fought for our country, and now, in our pain, it felt like our country was fighting against us. In essence, the government said to veterans that it was not the government's responsibility and basically abandoned its veterans.

Recalling feelings in the years after returning, Bob Nichols says, "Vietnam was a political war. I had respect and trust for the politicians who ran the war. However, I became so disillusioned that I look back and see them as slightly below whale shit lying on the bottom of the deepest part of the ocean." Strong words, yes, but true feelings from one who went through hell.

Some of us were so disillusioned by the way we had been treated that we wanted nothing to do with the government. Mitch Perdue had a variety of physical problems and says, "I vehemently refused to go to the VA, regardless of the fact that I was entitled to care. For years, I wanted nothing to do with them."

Even issues like the effects of Agent Orange were denied for many years by the VA. While it was finally acknowledged that Agent Orange was a fatal problem, it was and still is underresearched and underfunded. As deadly as bullets, Agent Orange is a vicious killer even now, four decades later. A line in the very funny play *Greater Tuna* goes like this: "I hired fourteen Vietnam veterans. They were all good workers. Only five of them died though, and none of them even turned orange." Funny? To others, maybe yes. Funny to combat veterans? Hell, no!

Most of the American public saw only the sometimes strange and misunderstood behaviors of youngsters returning from combat. Americans have generally been sanitized from the reality of trauma. Most cannot stand the sight of blood, or of an automobile accident, or even of a pet being killed in the street. There are extreme fears that someone will break into our home. Yet as youngsters right out of school, we were trained as killers, sent into combat, and faced the uncertainty of life daily. Because we were betrayed on many fronts, many veterans emotionally isolated and withdrew into ourselves. Many of us also became hobos emotionally and some physically.

In 1972, Ray Shurling learned that the army was again opening up warrant officer flight school training. He applied and passed everything except his hearing tests. His hearing had been damaged firing the 106mm recoilless rifle in combat. As a result, he was not selected and in turn decided to file a disability claim with the VA.

> The doctor who examined me gave me a very hard time and asked endless questions about why I did not wear hearing protection in combat. I tried very hard to explain to the doctor that you can't call a time-out in combat so that you can put in earplugs. He refused to understand that you don't just run to your position at a 106mm recoilless rifle and look for ear pro-

tection while mortar rounds are falling all around you. He was adamant that I failed to follow army regulations and therefore the problem was my own fault. Later, I appeared before the VA claims office and there was more of the same. I was again grilled on why I did not wear hearing protection and my failure to follow army regulations was my fault. Neither of these people had a clue about combat. Their position was that getting shot at is no excuse for not wearing ear protection.

Just recently, Ray initiated another claim with the VA for his hearing. This time, his claim was approved after a hearing test and no questions were even asked about his "failure to follow army regulations" by the claims officer.

Little was readily available in the way of help or an understanding of how Vietnam returnees were treated. However, there were some efforts, as seen in an article in the *Atlanta Constitution* dated October 20, 1969, written by Alfred A. Messer, MD, who was identified as an expert in family counseling and professor of psychiatry at Emory University. Dr. Messer's article offered some ways of understanding and helping returning GIs with their readjustment.

Thankfully, in recent years, much of this has changed favorably with the government and the American public. Probably one of the indirect results of 9/11 is that the American public finally seems to be getting a slight hint of the reality that trauma changes people forever. Terror is not just thousands of miles away. We are no longer sanitized from the reality of trauma. The collective guilt of America for Vietnam veterans over what was not done or not being done gradually made our society and our government realize the neglect that many combat veterans had experienced.

Time has made a difference. Our anger and resentment over how we originally were treated has not gone away. However, we can say strongly and unequivocally that our nation is still the greatest country in the world. Help is now available via the VA, and that is wonderful. And in spite of our lingering pain from combat, we did as President Kennedy asked and proudly "did for our country."

III

LIVING WITH OUR TRAUMA—
EVER-PRESENT SYMPTOMS

Little does anyone know of the physical damage combat does unless they have been in the midst of horrifying ambushes and firefights. What is known even less is the emotional damage resulting from combat. What has been written prior to the last few years has, for the most part, been much sanitized. Everyone has at least one friend, family member, neighbor, coworker, or acquaintance who has been traumatized. What is not known, however, are the inner wounds that occurred, which the traumatized person continues to experience.

To see or talk with any of us sixteen, you would see what most would describe as typical Americans. We have families, have (or had) careers, and have been successful in life in many ways. What you don't see is what each of us has been carrying around inside for four decades: a burned, torn, battered, and traumatized soul. Even our best friends and loved ones have seldom or never seen or have been aware of the depth of our symptoms. "He never talks about the war" is a comment often voiced. Some of us are now revealing, for the very first time ever, feelings and experiences that have been like demons and have haunted us for the past four decades.

In Vietnam, we were blindsided by ambushes, snipers, booby traps, rocket-propelled grenades, and mortars. Today, we are blindsided by nightmares, flashbacks, anger, depression, anxiety, guilt, and many other symptoms of our trauma.

You see, we all have become just as good at covering up our damaged insides as we were at being killing machines in combat. So the following symptoms, feelings, and behaviors that we sixteen experience are shared as very private, transparent, and personal parts of our lives.

We want to make it very clear that the trauma symptoms described in the following pages in no way serve as reasons or excuses for deviant or criminal behavior.

7

SLEEP PROBLEMS AND NIGHTMARES

All sixteen of us have had difficulty with our sleep—not all the time and not always with the same intensity. But our combat trauma comes out for sure in our sleep, and in many cases in our lack of sleep.

Common are intrusive thoughts while trying to go to sleep. Minds rush with a flood of thoughts, and when the mental images of combat enter, often it is hours before sleep comes as our mind may traverse from one firefight to the next. When sleep does come, the intrusion may come out in dreams or nightmares. Vigilance often invades our sleep. Hundreds of times, we have awakened wet with sweat. It is very common in a nightmare to feel frozen or paralyzed, where we can't move, fight, run, or retreat.

In recent years, I have had numerous dreams of violence. Since I am not a violent person, these dreams are troubling. One dream is of an attacker, not in Vietnam, who is attempting to shoot me. I wrestle the pistol away and shoot the attacker twice. As the attacker is lying on the ground, I shoot him four more times. I awaken with severe guilt. Another dream is of me attacking an antagonizer. I am hitting him with my fists attempting to do serious harm. The antagonizer retreats, only to return. I have a pistol and fire three rounds at him, missing. In the dream, I am angry at myself for missing.

These are troubling dreams for me, as I am very peace loving. The last real fight I had was as a nineteen-year-old football player at Wake Forest when I had a post-play fight in practice with another teammate. It is confusing, being nonviolent, for these dreams of violence to be so frequent, and my subconscious homicidal aggression is troubling.

Many times I awaken in the middle of the night feeling very anxious and unable to return to sleep. These lonely hours are usually spent with entangled thoughts and feelings about Vietnam. I am left exhausted the next day, which causes depressed moods that sometimes last all day. I am angry that I have mortgaged a portion of my earlier life and am now paying the emotional interest and principal.

A continuing dream for me is of being with my men when a firefight begins and we are about to be overrun by the enemy. Being a chaplain, I never went into combat carrying a weapon. I saw my role to minister to my soldiers prior to and in the midst of combat. In the dream, I feel helpless and immobilized. I always awaken terrified.

The battle of Snoopy's Nose is a dream that I have had probably over a hundred times. I see the boats on fire, the explosions all around, hear the small-arms fire hitting the sides of the boats, and see the blood-covered well deck of the navy ATC that wiped out one of Company A's platoons with a B-40 rocket. I am frantically trying to patch up the wounded, but I feel helpless in this dream as so many are wounded.

Tony Normand was very new in his tour, as both of us went to Vietnam on the same plane. He became a platoon leader and initially served with the much-respected company commander Joe Jenkins. They were on patrol via a small navy boat when a small, crude enemy grenade bounced off the side of the boat and failed to explode. Just as they sped away, they were hit by a rocket-propelled grenade that did explode and went through both sides of the boat, blowing out both of Tony's eardrums and sending his helmet flying into the stream. Joe was yelling, but Tony, of course, could not hear due to his ear injury.

Later, Tony would tease Joe as to why Joe was hollering *after* the grenade and not before, and he would jokingly ask Joe if it was because he had something about white guys. (Joe is black.) Joe would always mumble something under his breath about "Just one" and keep walking with a faint, sly smile.

Tony still has dreams of that day. "In sleep, I see that stupid crude grenade coming toward me, and the explosion that soon followed. I wake up as Joe starts yelling and I sit up in the bed sweating with pulse racing." Strangely, in the dream, Tony always sees the rocket and sees Joe's lips moving as he is hollering. However, he never dreams of the humor that followed; he remembers that only when he is awake.

"Road Runner" operations were almost nightly for Tony's unit on Highway #4, which ran from Saigon deep into the Mekong Delta. To Tony, these runs made absolutely no sense, as the VC had no vehicles anyhow. "All we did was to be moving targets in the night for the VC to target practice." On one run, Tony's unit was ambushed. He was so angry that he fired all his ammunition long after the enemy had disengaged. He kept everyone else firing long afterward and Tony actually took over a machine gun and fired and fired.

> I still wake up firing that machine gun in total anger. I am wet with sweat and even find myself having to wipe away what seems like millions of imaginary gnats and mosquitoes swarming around my head and flying into my eyes and up my nose as I fire. My trauma is not the ambush per se, but rather the trauma of living with the totally unnecessary suffering and death.

The most dramatic event that causes recurring nightmares for Tony occurred in November 1967 in the Plain of Reeds. Landing by assault helicopters, Tony, the company commander, found himself amid a lot of incoming fire. Water was three to four feet deep, and enemy small-arms fire was crackling through the thick grass that was six to eight feet high.

> Each time you moved, the grass cut your skin like honed little knives. There was no place to take cover. Fire could not be returned because we could not see where to fire. I thought at the time that the recesses of hell could be no worse. I heard occasional shouts from a couple of the shorter guys where water was nearly over their heads. We were taking wounded, but couldn't get a medevac chopper in. One chopper attempted to hover in the deep grass to pick up one young wounded soldier. It was hit by enemy fire and lurched upward in a cloud of smoke and then veered rapidly towards the ground some distance from us, crashing and burning.

We kept inching forward. A soldier next to me was shot in the hand, but I had no way to get him out. Our medic bandaged the wound but he continued to bleed heavily. Another soldier helped him maneuver through the mud, water, and other hellish landscape. Suddenly, we came to some berms, but every time any of us got out of the water on the berms, sniper fire against us became more intense.

I called in air bursts of artillery and some of my soldiers were hit by stray fragments. Totally exhausted and mentally fatigued, we continued to move. A heavy burst of enemy small-arms fire came in on us from very nearby. Water was sprayed around us and the small-arms fire began to clip the grass off at head level. It was a choice of stay put and surely die or charge the guns and probably die, but with at least a chance to eliminate some of the bad guys. Heavy fire was now going both ways, and bullets were missing all of us by inches. We heard a loud, agonizing scream. At least one of those bastards would never shoot at us again.

Just then, I took a step onto the edge of a berm and saw the end of a rifle rising toward me just a few feet away. It was like slow motion as multiple rounds impacted my body bringing on total numbness, like being hit with a giant hammer over and over. The force of the rounds pounding into my flesh sent me flying backward, landing in a small pig pen with about a foot of water. In my agony, I immediately hollered for my soldiers not to let me drown. Several held my head up from the water. I later learned that I had been shot six times.

I knew I had been hit bad but had no sensation of pain or location. I could not get up. I looked down and a soldier was holding my stomach and pushing a large bloody bandage inward to slow the bleeding and keep my insides where they belonged. Another was stuffing part of his shirt into a hole in my back. My mind was racing to comprehend events and responsibilities. I faintly asked my radio operator to get my first platoon leader, Mike Becraft, on the radio. I tried to speak slowly and without emotion to explain what had happened and to tell him to take charge of the company.

The guys then laid me on top of a berm. I asked my radio operator to report to Lt. Becraft. He squeezed my hand and left. I knew no help could possibly come, and he and the others knew the same. I thanked the guys around me as I was becoming increasingly faint and could no longer hold consciousness. I looked up into the clouds as long as I could before my eyes finally closed to die.

I don't know how long I was unconscious, but suddenly, I awoke violently. I was several hundred feet above the ground, totally confused and disoriented, lying in a helicopter. A round of ground fire had just smashed through my right arm, which must have been hanging outside the open door. After this seventh time of being shot, I then faded away again and did not waken for over two days.

Tony had numerous surgeries and donated a kidney and other internal body parts to the garbage dump.

My first waking thought after this was that I was certainly going to die very soon. I could feel it and see it in the eyes of those who visited or treated me. Jim Johnson, my chaplain and good friend, visited me in the hospital, held my hand, prayed with me, all with tears in his eyes. He was also kind enough to write a letter to my wife, Claudia, back in the States. Shortly, another friend and former commander, Joe Jenkins, visited. Joe, a very tough and battle-hardened soldier who never showed emotion, glanced at me, turned his head, and then focused on the oxygen tent above my bed. He whispered to me, tried to make a couple of jokes, and slowly walked away, head down.

Miraculously Tony survived. For weeks, he lay near death in his hospital bed in Saigon and later in Japan—alone and without family or friend. He had become infected from the pig feces in the water that infiltrated his wounds after his body had been riddled with enemy bullets. He was very much alone, often with high fever, thinking he was dying and wondering if he'd ever see his wife, Claudia, and their child again. He was even placed in what Tony calls "the death ward" for the most critically wounded. Most of the wounded soldiers there died, and Tony made it his quest to get out of that ward. It would be many weeks before his trip home was completed.

Tony has a recurring nightmare of seeing that AK-47 suddenly rise above the berm and the VC firing those rounds into his body. The dream is always the same.

On day two after returning from Vietnam, Ray Shurling had his first nightmare.

My mother had never seen me "that way," and on one occasion a few days later after another of my nightmares, broke down in tears as she had watched me thrash about in the bed, calling out for things unknown. Before returning to duty, one night we talked until morning but I never told her of the horrors that I had been a part of. In April 2008, she was visiting me in my home and I had one of those nightmares, yelling, jerking about, and moaning. It was so loud that it woke her in the other end of my house. Coming to my bedroom, she yelled to awaken me. When I awakened, she said, "My God, that is the same dream you had when you got home from Vietnam." Only now does she know I have had them for thirty-eight years.

Many of the dream details are not remembered when awakened. But thrashing, screaming, and swinging are very common, making it especially frightening to a spouse. Ray Shurling's ex-wife and son were often terrified at night. When he had a nightmare, they were very careful not to touch him during the episode. In order to awaken Ray, they would get a broom to poke him because to be touched would trigger physical reactions. Numerous were the times that Ray's screams would fill the house.

Dreaming of being back in Vietnam for Ron Miriello causes him to awaken in sweat. He has learned, however, to awaken himself and be assured that he is in the peace and comfort of home, not on a gun mount on a floating target on a muddy Mekong Delta waterway.

Soon after getting out of the army in 1969, Roy Moseman began having nightmares. They became so bad that he dreaded going to sleep. He would intentionally get drunk nightly and pass out so he wouldn't have nightmares. Most of his nightmares are directly related to his being in Vietnam. A recurring dream is that he is in Vietnam and not supposed to be there but can't get anyone to understand that. He is called out on a mission but cannot find his gear. He is told to load up but knows if he goes out without his gear and M-16, he won't make it back alive. Sometimes he goes and encounters the enemy but his rifle won't fire or he can't find his ammunition. If Roy watches the news about current wars, nightmares will be frequent during the next few nights.

In Dave Schoenian's dreams, he is always being chased by the enemy and sometimes left behind, alone. His M-16 has no bullets. His dreams are brutal with lots of killing. He, too, used to drink himself to sleep. Now, when the nightmares begin, he just gets up after he awakens. The bed is always torn up and the pillows are soaked. His wife, Ella, cannot sleep with him as all night long, he is punching, kicking, and moaning. Most of the time, he doesn't remember the details of the dreams. The best sleep Dave gets is when his dog is nearby, helping guard the house, pulling her turn on guard while he sleeps.

A recurring dream for Bob Stumpf occurs when a "gook" walks up to him and shoots him in the face.

> I never get a chance to defend myself. When I awaken, the anxiety and pressure that I feel in my chest feels like I am having a heart attack. Many nights after this dream, I am unable to go back to sleep. Sometimes I drift off by imagining myself back in the rice paddies with my platoon and for some reason this calms me. I am with my brothers, who I know will protect me!

Bob cannot sleep more than a few hours at a time. He wakes up sweating and his wife says his legs usually are moving like he is running.

Also haunted and tormented, Guy P. Moore wakes up sweating and confused, and he feels like his nightmare is very real and the trauma has just happened. His dreams of terror are very vivid. Guy sleeps only two to four hours per night because of the intrusion of his recurrent nightmares.

The lack of sleep or the troubling intrusions usually leave us fatigued the next day and that often leaves us feeling out of control and sometimes angry. Some of us are assisted by medications for sleep, but combat is always just a catnap away.

8

FLASHBACKS

In some ways, flashbacks are like nightmares, except that they occur while awake. Our flashbacks may be for just a fleeting moment or two, but they often impact us for an extended period of time. The flashback usually involves an episode of combat trauma, such as being wounded, seeing others wounded, sniper fire, firefights, major battles, preparing to go on a combat operation, being trapped and unable to move, and so on.

Due to a blood disorder that makes keeping the clotting balance difficult, I was recovering in the hospital after some relatively minor surgery. My physician was keeping me in the hospital for several extra days for observation until my blood was clotting properly.

Two days post-op, I had unknowingly injured my shoulders trying to lift myself from a bedside chair. I thought little of it at the time. The next morning, as I was beginning to awaken, I wanted to raise the head of my hospital bed. I could not move! Both arms were completely immobilized and in attempting to move my arms the pain was all but unbearable! I was very near panic and immediately decided to call the nurse for help. However, I could not move either hand to the call button. I was flushed; my breathing became very rapid and very shallow. My heart rate jumped and I broke out in a sweat.

Immediately, I realized that these were the exact same circumstances as I experienced on March 1, 1968. I was with Company A when they were suddenly hit. I was blown into an empty canal with a severely damaged right shoulder that eventually would be surgically reconstructed. It was my last combat operation and during that ferocious firefight, my best friend, Frank Pina, and two other soldiers were killed. In that instant, lying in the mud, I was totally immobile while explosions and gunfire were going on all around me. I was absolutely petrified and all but passed out from the excruciating pain from my damaged shoulder. Even though I am fully recovered physically, my shoulder still has metal screws internally and my rotation movement continues to be severely limited.

Now, thirty-eight years later, my emotions were again exploding as I lay helpless in the hospital bed. I was sobbing uncontrollably. I was thankful that I had a private room and that the door was closed as I cried for several minutes. All the fear of 1968 was erupting in me like an emotional Mount St. Helens. I was gripped with an overwhelming sadness in remembering my dead buddy, Frank. There was some guilt, as my emotions were running amok, that I had made it home alive and Frank and so many of my other soldiers had not. And my shoulders remained immobile and extremely painful when I tried to move them.

Finally, a nurse came to my room and was shocked to see my condition. Through my tears and embarrassment, I had to tell her what was going on and that, as a result of my PTSD, my flashback was all but incapacitating me physically and emotionally. Some Librium and the on-call therapist were of great benefit to me the rest of the day, but my combat trauma was intensely with me for the next several days.

Another time, I became stuck on an elevator in a hotel in Rome. Seven passengers were tightly packed in. Immediately I felt trapped, with the exact same feelings that occurred in the midst of an ambush. Heavy, shallow breathing and a pounding heartbeat were immediate. However, as in an ambush, I immediately realized that no one can panic and immediately took control, telling the two persons at the door to pry as hard as they could, telling the person in front of the control panel to keep pushing buttons, and telling the others to keep hollering for help in unison. Simultaneously, I surveyed the top of the elevator for a possible escape route, while self-talking myself to breathe deeply and slowly and not show panic to the other passengers. Help soon came but there was no emotional rescue for me from this "ambush."

One Saturday morning, Ray Shurling and I and a mutual friend were playing golf on a course at Fort Bragg, North Carolina. On the ninth tee, an old Huey helicopter from a nearby army airfield took off and flew very low overhead. It had a red cross painted on the side and looked exactly like the medevac choppers used in Vietnam. This old chopper was probably being flown by a reserve unit on weekend duty. No words were exchanged between Ray and me, but we glanced at each other.

As the chopper flew over the horizon, we played on to the tenth hole. On the green, the unmistakable "wop, wop, wop" of the chopper blades meant it was coming back over the golf course. Again, no words were exchanged, but we both walked to different sides of the green and pretended some trash was in our eyes. Our hearts were pounding, teeth clenched, and emotions were very raw—just like they were decades before. The rest of the round was terrible for each of us.

Clearly, mine and Ray's simultaneous flashback traversed many years, and just the sight of that red cross made the memory of so many wounded soldiers being evacuated come back very vividly. The next day, Ray e-mailed me and said,

> Saturday, when we were playing golf and stood on the #9 tee box, we heard the sound of a distant helicopter. We both knew it was an old Huey. As it flew over, I saw the pronounced red cross on the side. I suddenly was overcome with emotion. Obviously, you were as well. Inside my head I was hearing sounds from the past for a medevac . . . hot landing zone! The sound of a bullet ripping through the boom! Fear!! Then we made the turn to hole #10 and sure enough the medevac flew over again. More memories rushed in . . . we got the wounded aboard, the struts never touched the ground. The sounds of the chopper fade, the radio is quiet. We pull back. I have survived this day. . . . We both double bogie #10.

I phoned Ray and we were able to talk at length about what each of us had experienced the day before and were continuing to feel. It had taken decades to be able to talk about residual feelings that come as a result of seemingly benign events that cause those troubling flashbacks. Only two combat veterans could truly understand what had happened.

On another occasion, we were at the University of North Carolina Medical Center where Ray was to undergo an MRI, which he had never experienced. I was there with my buddy for moral support. Immediately, when placed in the machine, Ray felt like he does in one of his nightmares where he is trapped by the VC and cannot move. He couldn't breathe, his heart rate jumped, and he began yelling for help. In the next room, I clearly knew from his behavior that Ray was having a flashback. The attendants quickly extracted Ray, whose face was white as this paper and whose blood pressure had skyrocketed. Ray had a keen desire to run, but thought better of it as I guided him outside. Slowly, Ray returned to normal breathing, but he was bothered by this flashback for days afterward.

In 1972, John Iannucci picked up the magazine section of his Sunday newspaper and saw a photo of President Nixon placing the Medal of Honor on Thomas Kinsman, a former member of John's squad. Tom had done the unthinkable; he threw himself on a hand grenade that had been tossed into their position by the enemy. Fortunately, Kinsman lived, but he was horribly wounded with injuries that would affect him for the rest of his life. Upon reading the story of his hero friend, John flashed back and relived that terrible day for several weeks, day and night. He wanted to talk to someone about it, but had no one.

Roy Moseman has a small river that flows through his backyard. Sometimes he will be outside by the river and a UH1D helicopter from the National Guard unit will fly over. "No matter what I am doing, I sometimes feel that I am back in Nam and I am very aware of the chopper and I start watching the tree line on the other side of the river. I catch myself moving behind a tree for cover."

Ron Miriello recently watched a combat special on the History channel. After an hour of intense concentration, even though he was in the climate-controlled comfort of his recliner, Ron found himself sweating profusely. He had to leave and take a cold shower and get a change of clothing.

The firefight scene in the movie *Forrest Gump* had the same effect on both Roy Moseman and me. Roy began to shake all over and his heart rate became very elevated, almost making him leave the theater. I describe my flashback in my book, *Combat Chaplain*, as follows:

After the movie, I say nothing as we get into the car, nothing as we leave the parking lot, nothing as we drive toward the street. "Something about that movie bothered you, didn't it?" Barbara says. My scream is immediate. "I HATE THAT SHIT!!!" I'm shocked at my outburst. I begin to cry; can barely see through my tears enough to pull to the side of the street. I mumble more about hating "that stuff," and make little sense to Barbara. As I finally begin to calm down, Barbara asks, "What about the movie do you hate?" "That war shit. That ambush scene was just the way it was." . . . I'm aware that I'm tightly gripping the steering wheel. . . . The scene could have been any one of a score of firefights years before, and the sounds and sights depicted in that scene brought out feelings that crawled all over me like worms in a dead, rotting animal.

After seeing the movie *We Were Soldiers*, Roy left the movie without saying a word. "I was affected for several days from seeing this movie and had several nights of nightmares."

A number of years ago, Charlie Taylor was on a trip to South China. He took a tour of the countryside. Once in the country, there were rice paddies, conical straw hats, and tree lines. Embarrassed, Charlie sat on the floor of the bus to avoid seeing out. "My emotions raged."

In addition to the nightmares, the day Tony Normand was shot seven times is flashed back over and over. He sees the rifle on the other end of the berm rising and feels the thuds and burning as the rounds tear into his body. The fear of drowning and then realizing he is abandoning his troops is as real as it was four decades ago.

Flashbacks can occur even during times of joy, which can rob a combat trauma victim of current enjoyment. Recently, Ray Shurling experienced the birth of his first grandchild. For several days pre- and post-birth, Ray had been on a tremendous emotional high. Then he sent the following e-mail to me:

Padre, I am so angry, very angry! So angry that I will say f--- that war. So mad I want to lash out at the enemy, the VC . . . whoever, whatever. Damn this all to hell. Yesterday I went to the hospital to visit my grandson. The hospital evac chopper was quietly sitting on the pad. When I walked out, I stared at the chopper. [In 1969 some Vietnamese kids and their mothers were scrounging in a garbage dump. An old mine exploded under them with dozens killed and injured. Ray and his buddies called in choppers to airlift the injured children and mothers to a hospital. This horrible scene has been seared on Ray's soul for four decades.] Suddenly the chopper was surrounded by the Vietnamese trying to get their children on the chopper. But, this time it was different. . . . I was not helping them. I was in the crowd. It was me trying to get my grandchild on that chopper. The screams and horrible look on the faces of the parents . . . crying children . . . the sting on my face from the dirt whipped up by the chopper blades . . . the terrible helpless feeling when the chopper had to leave some behind. This scene was as real in my mind as the real event thirty-eight years ago.

By the time I got to my truck, tears were on my cheeks. By the time I got home I was full of anger, perhaps rage. I wanted to fight back, but fight who . . . fight what? If some fool driver had cut me off in traffic, I could have easily smashed into them on purpose. Why angry? This craziness has robbed me, stolen a moment of joy from me. Thoughts that invaded space reserved only for my newborn grandson and I hate that.

Flashback? Yes, in the most vivid detail, Ray's emotional transportation back four decades left him quivering with rage and feeling that the dramatic mine explosion then blew up in his emotional face. So sad, but so real.

Flashbacks are a real part of our memories and our memories contain so much pain from the exposure we had four decades ago. Like a bolt of lightning, a flashback can instantaneously transport us back to any rice paddy, any gunshot or B-40 rocket round, or any sight of torn flesh—or, worse still, the very still corpse of a buddy who has just been killed.

As is the case with all of our flashbacks, the historical event is not just remembered; rather it is relived as the terror, grief, anger, sadness, and horror are all mixed together.

9

TRIGGERS

For one who has not experienced combat terror and trauma, the following might seem to be very benign and meaningless. However, to us, so many events and situations can immediately trigger a sharp feeling and in some cases an unanticipated and unwanted reaction. Many sensations such as smells, sounds, sights, and tastes can send us back four decades in the blink of an eye. Resultant arousals are not necessarily incapacitating but are troubling.

Triggers are different, though, from flashbacks and nightmares in that triggers are just that: something is triggered from our past that immediately creates discomfort emotionally and sometimes physically and relationally. A trigger usually does not cause extensive preoccupation or disruption in what we are doing in that it is usually a fleeting sensation, albeit still discomforting. Nevertheless, triggers take us directly to a historical source of pain.

A recall that is triggered can result from a conversation, from a media event, or from some completely unknown source. It may appear to "just happen," with no known conscious cause. Yet, all triggers have a historical source for us in some way.

Recently, a friend of mine found the grave site of Larry Garner, better known as "Bandido Charlie" to the soldiers he commanded in 1967.

He was a very brave and respected leader who was killed shortly after my arrival. He also was Charlie Taylor's company commander. A copy of a photograph of Larry's grave triggered many sad feelings for me the day I received it.

A Vietnamese food market in Louisiana caused Terry Gander to leave immediately. The smell and the sights were more than he could handle emotionally.

Movies such as *Forrest Gump, Platoon, We Were Soldiers*, and *Hamburger Hill* trigger many feelings. So do *Saving Private Ryan, Patriot, Cold Mountain*, and even *The Passion of the Christ*.

Memorial services are especially trigger prone. Yet, some of us are involved in these frequently. I have conducted many over the years. Dave Schoenian does an "empty chair" ceremony that represents both those killed in action and those missing in action. Each time we participate in a service, we are left emotionally drained and wrung out. Yet, there is a continuing healing "salve" that comes from these services.

Bob Nichols is a bugler and plays taps at memorial services. Hearing taps for some of us requires nerves of steel to hold our composure, yet there is usually a mix of sadness and pride. Roy Moseman even has a recording of taps that he plays over and over in private because the beauty of the notes seems to soothe his negative memories. Still, taps is a very powerful trigger. Taps tends to make Frank Martinolich angry, "not just for the buddies who were lost so needlessly, but also for the indifference some show towards them."

The very mention of the name Jane Fonda will quickly trigger the raising of the blood pressure of a roomful of vets. She is probably the most hated celebrity and attracts many very uncomplimentary comments from those of us who served in combat. Rightly or wrongly, she is seen as a traitor and one who by her insensitive actions in going to Hanoi caused additional casualties to our brothers.

Many of us are somewhat apolitical, but the mere mention of certain politicians who were supposedly "combat decorated" can trigger very intense feelings. Many of us who served with young wannabe politicians who used what we consider our brothers' blood and valor for their own political aggrandizement consider this at best shameful and at worst treachery.

Seeing a wreck, smelling gunpowder or sulfur, hearing a "boom box," hearing the national anthem, seeing a TV image of combat, or even Veterans Day events can trigger trauma symptoms in many of us.

One of the most powerful triggers for those of us who were in the Mobile Riverine Force is the smell of diesel fuel. With every smell, we can picture ourselves loading into an ATC (Tango boat) off the side of the pontoon, listening to the slow rumbling idle of the diesel engine and smelling the exhaust fumes from the boats. Anxiety can be momentarily overwhelming because four decades earlier, loading onto the boats meant that we could very well be in combat shortly.

The smell of diesel fuel is constant on highways from semitrucks, at gas stations, in many workplaces, and even at fun places like county fairs where machinery may operate on diesel fuel. For many years, Bob Stumpf did not understand why the buses caused him so much discomfort when he rode one to work in New York City. It almost always made him sick, causing him to feel anxious and nervous. At times, Bob would have to prematurely exit the bus. He finally associated the smell of the diesel fuel with the Tango boats.

Of course, once off-loaded from the boats, we were *always* in water within a short distance from landing. We stayed wet until the operation ended, as water was everywhere. Periodically, the drain in the shower of Erol Tuzcu's home would temporarily clog. Standing in the water, even if it was only backed up just an inch or so, would drive him nuts. It was much later in his life that he finally realized that standing in water was a powerful trigger to his miserable past in the wet hell of the Mekong Delta.

The sight and thought of ants trigger very intense feelings in Frank Martinolich. On June 19, 1968, two days after Frank turned twenty, following an air strike on several enemy positions in bunkered positions,

> several of us were sent to check out the damage. Lt. Oakes was up front, followed by Ron Honeycutt, me, and then Platoon Sgt. Jon Winger. Winger moved ahead of me just as the enemy opened up from a bunker directly in front of us. Oakes was killed, Honeycutt was hit in the chest and lost an arm, and Winger took nine rounds from his neck to his waist and fell alongside me as I dove down. I had a very small neck wound. I threw all of my grenades and then got the grenades from Winger's dead body and threw them, too.

After contact was broken, we evacuated the bodies and wounded and then began moving to be extracted, when we walked into still another ambush. Fire was coming from all sides and was fast and furious. Most of our remaining platoon was pinned down. Three of us laid down fire so the rest of the platoon could make a run for cover. As we did, our machine gunner was hit in the head and I grabbed him and brought him to my lap and took a small towel and applied pressure to his wound until the medic came. The three of us who were left were the last to pull back. As we were laying down more protective fire, a helicopter fired a rocket at the three of us, mistaking us for the enemy. The rocket landed next to me and blew me several feet. Burning metal was all around me. In the midst of all the chaos, I suddenly realized that my legs were burning—I had been blown into a bed of ants that were biting and stinging me. I have relived this countless times since.

A short time later, being third in line on a five-man reconnaissance team did not save Frank, as three of the five were wounded by a booby trap. Frank had a hole in his left side, two holes in his back hip, and hundreds of small holes in his legs and arms. Later the doctor removed half a baggie full of metal from the larger wounds but had to leave many of the smaller pieces of metal.

Charlie Taylor visited Mazatlan, Mexico, on vacation once. The smell of the tropics, the decaying jungle, and especially the diesel fuel from the trucks made him literally sick and very uncomfortable.

We live with daily triggers that cause temporary negative associations with our combat trauma of four decades ago, trauma that is permanently etched in our memories and will be there until we die.

⑩

WITHDRAWAL, NUMBNESS, AND DEPRESSION

WITHDRAWAL

When a child is scolded, hurt, or sad, the child's natural tendency is to go to a corner or to another room and be alone until the feelings subside. Normally, this happens within a few moments. For combat trauma victims, there is also a natural tendency to withdraw. Unfortunately, instead of a few moments, our withdrawal may last days, weeks, and in some cases a lifetime.

Some of us do not risk making very close friends because of the threat of losing them. Deep inside, there is the fear that they might get killed, and that just hurts too much. We all lost so many friends four decades ago. Plus, the message that society and our government gave us—correctly or incorrectly—was that none of that mattered. This has confused us, as it makes absolutely no sense at our feeling level. Therefore, the natural tendency is to withdraw or isolate ourselves.

In suppressing or repressing our feelings, it often has seemed like we became stuck in our past. With no way to adequately deal with our histories, unfortunately these feelings come out in nightmares as well as in relationships with others.

Very soon after returning from Vietnam, I realized that emotionally, I must stuff my feelings. There was no one with whom to discuss what had happened to me, as most of the other people at my new assignment had no idea what it was like to live the life of a grunt daily. Fearing that if I said anything, I would be discounted and seen as just "war-storying" to get one up on others, I just shut up for several decades. When faced with the unpleasantness of my past combat trauma and knowing others had no idea or interest in it, I developed a fantasy of just going somewhere else and leave the unpleasantness behind.

The lost 1970s for John Iannucci involved more and more anger at the way the Vietnam War ended. He was very ashamed that our government had allowed so many thousands of American youth to die and be maimed, only to abandon South Vietnam and leave them to that horrible end. Not understanding what it was all for, John alienated himself more and more from family and friends. He lived each day without drive or motivation, just going through the motions.

While not ashamed of having been in Vietnam, John Adame was very careful whom he told about it. He shared little information, even with his family and friends. In fact, for many years he stayed walled off from those who wanted to be close. This withdrawal really began for him after that terrible experience of April 7, 1968. "Everyone seemed to get killed that I got close to. So, I just learned to keep my distance in order to protect myself from more loss."

"Disconnect" is the word that Frank Martinolich has heard for years from professionals. He has pushed his feelings down so deeply that he feels numb. In relationships, he cannot share himself the way others would normally expect him to. His fear is that if he reveals anything of himself to someone who wishes to get closer to him, he'll become vulnerable. Because his underlying anger is so strong, he usually will just shut down, which leads to a deterioration of the relationship. "I don't have any emotional attachment once it is gone. It is just like dealing with things in Vietnam—deal with it at the moment, be satisfied, and move on."

After the battle on February 26–27, 1968, Guy P. Moore had lost so many friends that he feels he was never "right in the head" again. He became a loner and had no desire to make new friends or ever get close to anyone again. This has carried over for him until just a few years ago, when he reconnected with many of the rest of us who served with him.

Roy Moseman learned very early after his return from Vietnam to turn off emotions in a second. "When things get bad I turn them off. My family thinks that I don't care, but it's my way of handling it. I will completely shut out the problem until I am alone and can rationally think about how to handle it." Roy's son recently left for Afghanistan. "Rather than getting real upset, I have gone into that 'protective mode' and cut off my emotions. It's like I do not believe that he is there. It still has not hit me as to how dangerous my son's assignment might be."

Hiding was a theme for Mitch Perdue. He refused to attend family reunions, without understanding why. Of course, others did not understand either. Likewise, Dave Schoenian came home to learn that "Vietnam" was a dirty word. Finally he just quit talking about it to those who were not veterans.

A refusal to develop close relationships or running away from the ones he has is a continuing theme for Ray Shurling. For the past fifteen years, he and I have been absolutely the best friends possible. We are even more like brothers than friends. Yet in 2005, I developed kidney cancer, resulting in the removal of one kidney. During my initial recovery, Ray was very attentive. Then there were additional, unexpected complications and surgeries that resulted in my being in a coma and on a respirator for several days. Mysteriously, Ray withdrew. It was a couple of weeks later that Ray was able to put together why he had withdrawn from me, his best friend. "I thought you were going to die, and I didn't know how to deal with your death except to do what I had done for years and that was to withdraw." Once he realized what he was doing, Ray apologized many times. Yet his withdrawal was an immediate reaction to what many of us did years ago, in that we did not want to experience additional death and loss.

Crowds spook Bob Stumpf. He avoids busy shopping centers. He even had a difficult time staying in the reception room during the weddings of his children. In fact, when it was time for photos, they had to go outside and get him.

Many times after a particularly traumatic firefight when people were lost, a common expression used by many grunts was "It don't mean shit" or "F--- it all." For a young soldier, to lose a good friend meant losing a part of oneself, and not having time or the means to make sense of the loss simply caused us to go into a corner or another room. It seemed then and now to be the only way to cope.

Unfortunately, withdrawal does not make our pain go away.

NUMBNESS

If we live long enough, every adult sooner or later will experience an event or series of events that could cause one's feelings to be severely blunted. Usually, though, this blunting of feelings is very temporary. But for the combat trauma veteran, it is not unusual for one's emotions not only to be numb, but to remain so for years and maybe even for the rest of one's life.

Our memories of so many traumatic events create in some of us a disengagement of human emotion. During combat, that disengagement often saved lives, including our own. It certainly helped us to maintain mental stability. But the survival mode that enabled us to turn off our feelings four decades ago now can keep us from being connected to others in loving, nurturing ways, and this we sincerely regret.

When one's physical nerve endings have been burned, painful stimuli are blocked. When one's emotional "nerve endings" have been severely damaged, not only pain and sadness but joy can also be blunted. Seeing so many wounded and killed caused us to become very callous and often left us without many positive feelings. Therefore, suppression of emotions became one way of trying to cope with our terrible memories. Unfortunately, this mechanism was not left in Vietnam.

"Callous" is how Bob Nichols felt for many years after his combat trauma.

> I lost my emotions. I had no feelings at funerals. My grandmother died, and I loved her, but there were no tears. My mother-in-law died in 1982, and again I shed no tears for this good woman. Vietnam had blunted my feelings. Now, in later years, my feelings are changing. I am finally becoming more feeling now than I was in those post-Vietnam years.

It is very frustrating for Frank Martinolich to have no emotions.

> I am emotionally numb. I lost any ability to cry, have no clue to internal feelings, don't like to be hugged. I have been told by professionals that I have intellectual emotions but other than anger, I have no internal feelings. I don't know how to mourn, be happy, sad, or know how to love. I feel disconnected. I have that empty tank.

Before going to Vietnam, Roy Moseman was an easygoing, fun-loving person with lots of different emotions.

After Vietnam, I went for years without emotions. Nothing made me happy and nothing made me sad. If anything bad happened like a death in the family, I would just turn my emotions off. I guess people thought I didn't care—and at the time I didn't, but that was my way of handling it. That's the way I handled death in Vietnam. I just turned off my emotions. If not, I would not have been able to survive.

"I have been accused more than once of being emotionally dead," says Ray Shurling. Likewise, Bob Stumpf pretty much shut down and feels that he was in shock a good part of the time after returning from Vietnam. In fact, he says,

I am still living in a state of numbness, going through the motions of life without feelings. At times, it is an emptiness that knows no bounds. All these years, I have felt emotionally crippled and stone-cold inside. I have alienated and pushed people away.

Being in a Vietnamese unit, Ray Shurling saw many die, but never an American. He coped by closing all feelings and emotions to the Vietnamese in his unit. "I had to convince myself that they weren't really like us, and if they died in combat, I was sorry, but I walled off my emotions that their lives really did not matter." In the ensuing years, Ray has continued to fight to correct these feelings.

Fortunately, now four decades later, some of the persons we can feel free enough to show our emotions with are other combat veterans. This brotherhood of trust has probably saved many of our lives, figuratively and literally.

DEPRESSION

"Blue Monday, how I hate Blue Monday" is a line from a song made popular by Fats Domino prior to the time we were in Vietnam. To be blue simply means to have a down day—a day when there is an element of sadness, a day when our mood is down. This is not the same as clinical depression, though. Combat trauma vets periodically suffer from both.

We probably experience more down days or "blue Mondays" than the average person. Simple triggers, as has already been mentioned, can cause us to feel down. It may be a blue Monday or any day. However, just a down mood is not lasting nor disabling.

What can be disabling, though, is the persistent sadness that some of us experience that results from the strong memories of combat, guilt, and unresolved grief over the loss of our brothers and even from the "loss of innocence" that many of us experienced with that first gunshot from the enemy.

Just prior to my having to cease work, my sadness began oozing out, often via tears at seemingly unprovoked times. This greatly worried me and, at times, was embarrassing to me. For over three decades, I had held it together, never daring to allow others to see the stored-up sadness I was experiencing inside. While I was not clinically depressed per se, my frequent down moods were of increasing concern to me, especially with my being a therapist. Fortunately, I finally had the good sense to bury my pride and denial, and I sought help via the VA.

Prolonged thoughts of traumatic events led Terry Gander to become clinically depressed. Fortunately, his physician had the good sense to hospitalize him and treat his depression.

In the early 1970s, John Iannucci's father died. This is the father who periodically sent John spending money to Vietnam because John's pay was messed up for the first seven months in country and John received no pay. John's father loved him deeply and John loved his father deeply. However, John was so depressed and sad that he went through the entire process of his father's death and funeral without outward emotion. He was like a robot. Someone asked a family member if John and his father were on bad terms, because it appeared that John was not affected by his father's death. What they did not know was that John's experience in combat had made him so emotionally empty that it was humanly impossible for him to outwardly express feelings.

For several years, Roy Moseman never cried, nor ever got excited about anything. "About the time I turned thirty or thirty-five, I became too emotional and now I cry at the drop of a hat, especially when it comes to Vietnam and veterans. I get embarrassed because I can hardly mention anything about Vietnam without tearing up. Medication is now helping with this."

Whereas anger has been a companion of Bob Stumpf, the depression resulting from his unresolved anger oftentimes leaves him cold inside.

He cannot relate to anyone, not even his family or even his wife during these periods. He describes these times as feeling "dead inside, times where I do not care about anything. These periods are unbearable, and I feel this way sometimes for days and weeks on end. I believe I will never feel happy and normal again, and I see the future as just a large empty void."

Every time Mitch Perdue thinks of an event of June 1, 1968, in Can Tho, he gets depressed and sad. Mitch was walking point.

> I just sensed something was wrong but could not pinpoint what it was. Something just didn't seem right. Lt. Yount ordered me to move faster because we had to get to an objective and were behind schedule. Also sensing something was not right, Yount went by me to check. Then all hell broke loose. Yount was immediately shot, losing his leg. The medic just behind me got hit. I crawled to help him as Sgt. Campbell crawled by me to see about Yount. Just as Campbell slithered past me, an AK-47 round slammed into his head right between the eyes. It was a terrible sight. Yount's bullet was for me, had I not sensed something was wrong. Then, in the midst of the firefight, Campbell's bullet would have been for me. I still think about this daily. It still hurts and sometimes I'm like in a trance.

Erol Tuzcu continues to have raging periods of sadness when he recalls an event of February 20, 1969, in Kien Hoa Providence. A/3/60th flew on what was thought to be a routine mission. As the helicopters dropped the troops, the landing zone proved to be very hot as the enemy opened up from several sides. Erol says,

> The feel, sights, and smells and the horror that occurred after we landed was to be with me the rest of my life. Several 105mm rounds had been rigged as booby traps and each time one would explode, several brothers would be hit. My buddy Mirick was walking point and tripped one of the rounds, blowing off both of his legs. I applied tourniquets and continued to dodge bullets but Mirick bled to death with me lying next to him with absolutely nothing I could do to save him.

Nothing can quell the feelings of having such a good friend die in your arms and you cannot save him.

Bob Nichols of B/3/60 was in the same firefight.

We were ambushed from a hooch. A VC battalion got the drop on us and our commander mistakenly headed in the wrong direction and we went into a dreaded L formation that the enemy had set up. The cross-fire against us was withering. We took many, many casualties that night. Dropped napalm lit up the sky like oil tank explosions. Tracers filled the dark sky. I can still sense the terrible smells of that battle. When the battle ended, not only had we lost a lot of good men and the VC were hit very hard, a stark memory is of a civilian woman who had been trapped between the two forces lying on her back covered in blood.

Not a day goes by but that each of us has something to remind us of our trauma. When a buddy has a limb shot off, or is blown apart by a booby trap, or has his entrails exiting from open wounds, or is wheezing because blood begins to block his airways, or has his brain matter coming out from where his ear once was, or is crumpled, still, and very dead, our sadness is ever present. We each have a life sentence that we have to accept, even though we certainly do not like it.

Not unlike a very low-grade fever, our down moods, sadness, and/or depression can degrade our daily lives by causing our joy to be ever so slightly minimized. But, we keep trying.

11

FEAR AND ANGER

FEAR

Fear was always present on every operation. The unknown of what was hidden on any stream bank or behind any nippa palm branch or in any tree line kept our stomachs tight with anxiety. Looking death in the eye daily was a very heavy load for any young person to endure.

All was quiet on the waterway but, as always, when the navy boats are moving, everyone was on alert for a possible ambush. Ron Miriello says,

> Our boat was cruising at the maximum speed of 8 mph and I was in my .50 caliber gun mount. Suddenly, we were under heavy small-arms and rocket fire from the nearby jungle. I began firing rounds as fast as I could, scared shitless, watched a B-40 rocket land close to my mount, then a second one closer. I knew death was facing me in the eye if a third round continued to be zeroed in on me. Out of nowhere, an F-4 Phantom jet dropped a five-hundred-pound napalm bomb on the enemy positions. I felt the heat and it was one beautiful sight. I owe my life to that pilot.

Ron also says that on that day, he was wearing flip-flops in the gun mount because he was having foot problems. The clang-clang of hot empty machine gun shells bounced off his bare feet, and with each bounce the skin was burned—but he knew he had to keep on firing.

Being one of only two Americans with a Vietnamese unit, Ray Shurling, at age twenty-one, bore the brunt of responsibility for not only himself but for the Vietnamese as well. During a withering firefight, Ray was firing as rapidly as his M-16 would allow. Ray called in artillery and suddenly realized he heard no other firing from his nearby positions. It was then that his adrenaline suddenly turned to monumental fear as he realized to his horror that all the Vietnamese soldiers had literally run away in retreat and he was the only friendly still fighting the onslaught. Ray was finally able to extract himself. Being alone and fighting off the enemy could have easily gotten him wounded or killed. He would have been left to die and his body to be mutilated by the enemy or to rot in the jungle. For his actions, Ray was awarded the Bronze Star for valor but his fear at being left alone in a firefight is to this day overwhelming.

The jumble of feelings that most of us experience changes from time to time, and the uncertainty of what we feel and why we feel it often causes us to fear that we might lose control. It's like being at the top of a waterfall, very close to the edge. At the bottom of the raging waters are the foam and rushing waters of rage, grief, fear, guilt, desperation, and the fear that we just might slip over the falls.

Some have felt that "if I talk about what is going on in my mind, I'll go crazy, and if I go crazy, it'll be the end of me." Fighting to control our feelings is an ongoing battle. Dave Schoenian once told his doctor that he was near crossing the line and if he did, there would be no coming back. He also feared that if pushed, he could even become homicidal.

"Often I find myself hanging on by my fingertips" is how Bob Stumpf describes himself. Especially after 9/11, which occurred near where Bob was working, he did not feel safe anywhere, nor did he feel safe inside himself with his feelings. He had increased difficulty getting along at work. As mentioned earlier, he actually got into a fistfight with a street person and literally threw him out the door of his bank building. The fact that the street person was wearing an old army jacket didn't help. Bob has gone through periods of dread for his children and grandchildren, of worry about losing his job or being killed in a wreck, and of expecting some disaster at work.

Charlie Taylor says, "I am more rigid than I need to be. But mistakes can get you killed. I saw it happen numerous times in Vietnam. You must remember what was taught you. All it takes is one mistake and you can be dead."

Erol Tuzcu is unable to let anyone have control of his business when he is away. "I do not take vacations or time off. I work twelve- to fourteen-hour days and half-days on Saturday and Sunday. I was never successful working for anyone else and always tried to place myself in a situation to maintain control."

Not only the *fear* of losing control but actually losing control can be emotionally devastating. A young army couple came to me for pre-marriage counseling. Both were officers and very much in love. A month after the wedding, a fiery wreck killed the new husband and severely injured his wife. I was so close to the edge emotionally that I could not minister to the young widow during her recovery in the hospital as I had for many others. I cried frequently, but no one knew but me.

Publicly, I did lose control at one of our staff retreats when I was suddenly and very unexpectedly immersed in feelings from Vietnam, resulting in my sobbing and pounding the table with my fists in the presence of other staff persons. Embarrassed and humiliated, it was as a result of this and other "close encounters" with losing control that I decided I must give up my career in a profession that I absolutely loved, else I could go over the edge.

But Terry Gander has said it best for us all: "It is most important for me to control it, not it to control me." Terry's statement is a keen desire for us all, but most times, this is easier said than done.

ANGER

Victims of combat trauma often experience and exhibit confusing anger that is not understood by others nor ourselves. While many of our emotions have been blunted, anger is one emotion that is very quick to surface for many of us. Our anger can be caused by something as benign as an everyday event that seems meaningless to someone else, or it can be the result of seeing 9/11 or the Virginia Tech massacre. It can be as a result of experiencing a Vietnam wannabe or a pretender who we know is dishonoring our lost buddies, or from any one of a thousand other stimulants.

We have much anger as a result of the injury and death experienced four decades ago. Having to keep all our feelings bottled up inside for all these years has made our anger continue to simmer, and it can erupt at any time—often at very inopportune times. Often, our anger is seen as having no apparent source.

In combat, anger was very common. The infantry soldier is trained to react quickly, and usually anger was an asset in a combat setting. It was part of the fight-or-flight syndrome that originated during caveman times when, faced suddenly with a saber-toothed tiger, one had to fight or flee. God made the human body so that, when the adrenaline pumps, one's blood vessels constrict and bleeding is minimized if the tiger attacks. The adrenaline helped the caveman deal with the immediate threat and gave him extraordinary strength. So too, in combat, the fear accompanying an ambush allowed us to do things we could never have done without the threat of being killed.

Clearly, when anger erupts, adrenaline and other chemicals enter the bloodstream, our heart beats faster, blood flows more quickly to the body, and muscles tense and strengthen. Also, the jaw may clench, palms get sweaty, breathing increases, and we may get flushed and talk loud. Now, four decades later, we know that anger causes stress, fear, frustration, disappointment, and even physical problems like headaches and gastrointestinal problems.

We see a very simple formula that addresses our anger. It looks like this:

Hurt or fear = anger

Anger is experienced as: rage, projection, or depression

Behind any of our anger is either hurt or fear and maybe both. Anger is like a fire, and our hurt or fear is like the fuel source for the fire. Unfortunately, stimulation of our hurt or fear can almost instantaneously produce the flame seen as anger, without us or others being aware that hurt/fear is what is actually behind our anger.

Our anger often is manifested in one of three ways:

1. **Rage** can be spewed onto others immediately. In an instant, we can verbally abuse a family member or a stranger. Rage may have no boundaries and can include physical violence.
2. **Projection** onto others may be much like the proverbial "kicking the dog" because something has not gone right earlier in the day.

3. **Turning our anger inward,** if done consistently, can cause depression and/or physical problems such as high blood pressure, heart problems, ulcers, and so on.

Four decades ago, we lived constantly with the fear of being wounded or killed and with emotional hurt from seeing so many of our brothers wounded or killed. This fear and hurt was not left on the other side of the world but remains a constant companion.

Our continual struggle is to experience our hurt/fear (anger) in *appropriate* ways, without hurting others or ourselves. This struggle is a lifetime endeavor for most of us. Many of us seek to monitor and control these feelings with the help of therapy, support groups, creative journaling, and finding ways to slow down our feelings to keep them under control. We often cause harm to others because of our anger, but that is not our intent.

Many of us remain very angry at our government for denying there was even a problem with any of us, especially pertaining to the lingering affects of PTSD. Plus, it was years before any acknowledgment was made that Agent Orange was a health problem. Now, thousands of our brothers have died as a result of exposure to Agent Orange. Each time another dies, we are collectively angered again but can do nothing about it. Then, the senselessness of so much of the flawed strategy in that war has left many of us deeply angry. The losses—for what?

Remembering the uselessness of those fearful "Road Runner" operations at night to keep the roads open south of Saigon caused much anger for Tony Normand then and now.

Those who survived that useless folly of keeping the road open at night when the VC didn't even have vehicles still makes me angry. The blood spilled there by good men is long forgotten by most. Over time the blood becomes covered in even deeper layers of dust thrown up by the passing traffic. The accumulated dust is as if to hide the evidence of fruitless decisions by those who should have known better.

Not having work clothes, Bob Nichols began working at his civilian job wearing fatigues (without patches). One of his supervisors was an E-6 in the reserves and made a nasty comment that he was an E-6 and Bob only made it to E-5. Bob immediately reacted in anger and told him where he could put his stripes—that "I got mine in combat." Fortunately, Bob was not fired.

During one firefight, several soldiers in John Adame's platoon were killed. A new platoon sergeant had just arrived, having been a drill sergeant in basic training. John was already angry at himself for not having been with these guys, as most of them were new. When the firefight ended, the new sergeant said, "Get those pieces of meat [the bodies] out of here." He never knew how close he came to being killed by Adame. "If I was to see him now, and we were in a room, one of us might not get out alive."

Guy P. Moore says he could easily write a book on his historical anger and rage.

> They have cost me dearly since Vietnam. I have been in jail many times for destruction of property and fighting when I lost control. I have taken out my anger on numerous innocent people. It was because I carried around a combat attitude and would react without thinking instead of rationally responding. That is exactly what I was trained to do in the army. I had no time to think through what was happening, only to react and usually violently.

Roy Moseman became a much angrier person, mad at the world sometimes, mad at everyone for no apparent reason:

> . . . mad at myself, even. I doubted myself for some of the things that I did in Vietnam. Some of the movies are so full of shit that it's a joke. I really get mad when I see how they portray the Vietnam soldier. I am sure there were some idiots in Nam who would do about anything, just like they are in any society, but I believe there were very few who would intentionally kill innocent civilians and children. It just didn't happen the way Hollywood wants the public to believe. We were not a bunch of drunken, pot-smoking idiots running around in the jungle killing people. I hate the people that live in this country enjoying their freedom but protest everything they can think of. At work, my biggest problem was always my outbreaks of anger. I would take things for so long and then I would explode. I would tell my boss what I thought of him and walk out the door. I would not take any verbal abuse. This is the main reason I opened my own company.

"The price paid for what?" Dave Schoenian says. "All the bullshit we put up with and how we were used as bait. Politics controls everything. The American public just doesn't get it and seems blind to everything."

Bob Stumpf says,

> Anger comes out of me for no apparent reason. I have broken things, punched walls and have acted like a total ass. I have a very short fuse. If someone bumps into me it takes a lot of self-control not to react. I was by nature a somewhat calm individual and did not usually look for trouble. My behavior disturbs me greatly. I had an incident on the bus where I got into a fistfight with someone who probably outweighed me by seventy-five pounds. Another time, I got into a fight with a NYC homeless street person who walked into our office at work. I have a lot of trouble dealing with the assholes of the world. I have no patience at all.

A series of events on March 16, 1968, in Can Tho created much fear and anger for Bob Stumpf then and now. Moving by ATCs on a canal, Bob's unit, Echo Company 3/60th, humped most of the day and only received sporadic sniper fire.

> Late in the afternoon, we were crossing a large paddy when we got hit with heavy automatic weapons fire and small arms from the wood line, pinning some of us down in the open paddy. Unfortunately our flanking platoon had gotten ahead of the rest of the company when the Cobra gunships came. I saw three brothers run into a hooch just before the Cobras launched their rockets. The Cobras, thinking the three were enemy, zeroed in on the hooch. These guys had no chance. The Cobras came around again and rockets landed so close to us this time that you could see the shrapnel shred some banana trees. I was actually picked up and dropped back into the canal by the sheer force of the explosions. My ears were ringing for days after. I was numb and in shock.
>
> When the fight was over and we checked the hooch, the carnage was unbelievable. One of our guys was almost cut in half. The other two were also dead. I cannot explain the horror of seeing this. I still smell the cordite and burned flesh as though it happened yesterday.
>
> We moved out. My buddy Abbot was walking point and I was second in the column. We were still in the canal with a dike and rice paddy on my right. Then we were hit again. We started receiving small-arms fire from the wood line. I had my M-16 over the top of the dike and was firing

into the wood line. I lost sight of Abbott as he crawled down the canal, and I did not see him again until he startled me as he grabbed my ankle. He was covered in mud and blood, having just been shot in the side. The only reason I didn't react and shoot him, thinking he was a VC, was that the dike prevented me from turning my weapon on him. I still think daily of how easy it would have been for me to have killed him, and I thank the Lord every day that I do not have to live with something like that.

Then, to make matters worse, our new platoon leader began shooting at me with an M-79 grenade launcher, thinking I was a VC. The asshole was popping them off at me from the rear. I can still feel those heat rounds landing around me. I had just nearly bought it from the Cobras and from the VC in the tree line, and now I had to worry about getting killed or wounded by this incompetent and candy-ass leader!!!

That night, as we set up our perimeter, another grunt and I were sent out on a listening post. I was scared shitless, expecting any moment to see a whole platoon of VC pop up in front of me. I have now been in Vietnam just a few weeks. How am I ever going to survive a whole year of this insanity?

As I mentioned earlier, shortly after returning to the States I had my shoulder rebuilt surgically due to the injury from my last firefight. Wearing a half body cast, for awhile I could not even feed myself. Absolutely humiliating was having to have my wife wipe my rear end when I went to the bathroom. I fought for weeks the dichotomy of anger at my condition and guilt that I only had a damaged shoulder when so many of my brothers returned home in a body bag. None of these feelings made sense to me.

Sometimes it is difficult to distinguish between our hurt and anger or when the hurt turns to anger. Recently, my wife and I were with another couple, who were longtime friends, at an entertainment event. A series of very well-done scenes involving the high cost of American freedom ended with a scene at the Vietnam Memorial Wall. Suddenly, I was having a flashback that triggered some very intense and embarrassing feelings.

In the car in the parking lot after the event, I was overcome with emotions, and suddenly found myself sobbing. I knew when I left the theater that I needed to get the feelings out, but since another couple was with us, I had no way to do that alone. My feelings during those moments were so intense that there was no way I could suppress them. I cried and babbled for probably fifteen minutes. As embarrassed as I was, and feeling trapped in the car, what I got from the female friend was certainly not what I needed. I got *absolute silence*! True, seeing me in that emotional state probably shocked her. But, not once did she in any way acknowledge the pain I was in. It was like "If I ignore him, it'll go away." Once again, four decades later, here was still another situation of "don't reveal your feelings," because being ignored when in such pain is probably worse than hostility. My hurt turned to very intense anger, but I in no way showed it. I just had to stuff it.

What if I had received a phone call that one of my children had been in a wreck? Or that our house had just burned down? Or that my wife or I had just been diagnosed with cancer? This female friend would have been very empathetic. Certainly, she would have never just ignored the bad news and made no reaction. Yet, the pain and anger that I was experiencing was very intense, but she made absolutely no acknowledgment of it in any way.

As I mentioned earlier, I resigned from my position of fifteen years, a position that I loved. Having spent my life helping others, I felt caught in an emotional bind due to the increasing negative effects of my trauma and felt that if I could not even help myself, how could I help others? Normally a very mild-mannered and in-control person, privately I experienced two episodes of absolute rage. I was never totally out of control, and it was in the middle of the night, but it did involve screaming, pounding the walls, and expressing rage. It was like a lifetime of pent-up feelings were bursting forth. Feeling safe in my own home, I did not try to quell the puking out of these feelings of anger and frustration.

Anger has caused some of us to make poor decisions at the wrong times, causing wrecks and road rage. It has hindered relationships by our insults, excessive criticizing, threatening, aggression, and verbal and physical assaults. Some of us have had fights with coworkers, family members, and in-laws.

It is never our intent to lash out at what at the time may seem to be unfair or unjust events. A part of our quest is to understand and control those historical hurts and fears that stimulate and feed anger because it hurts others and ourselves. None of us needs any more hurt to ourselves or our loved ones.

⑫

HYPERVIGILANCE, STARTLE, AND CONCENTRATION

HYPERVIGILANCE

Spending so much time in the jungle, sloshing across open rice paddies, riding exposed on boats to areas of operation, never knowing what or who might be waiting to kill us, we were trained to *always* be hypervigilant. Not to be vigilant could mean being killed or having a buddy killed. Being on constant guard did not cease when we landed in the States at tour's end. Awareness of our surroundings is still automatic. Feeling like we are always in possible danger or being always on alert for tragedy often takes its toll.

A tree line is an emotionally forbidden place for John Adame. He refuses to walk into any tree line. He also must have a night light on, because he wants to see what is around him immediately if need be.

There is constantly a newsreel-type of event going on in Frank Martinolich's head. This newsreel is from Vietnam and is for situations that come up, especially the unexpected ones. He is aware of multiple conversations simultaneously and can separate them. Frank sees all movement around him, no matter how subtle. Sudden noises will make him react.

Once a very trusting person who loved to be a part of a crowd, Ron Miriello is always very suspicious of whoever is nearby. When possible, he chooses not to be a part of a crowd. When he is in a crowd, he tries to position himself where he can see everyone. Having a line of sight and the best view of all entrance and exit locations is automatic.

Likewise, it is best not to get too close to Guy P. Moore unless you are one of his trusted friends. He, too, always has an exit plan in the event something happens.

In a restaurant or any other building, Roy Moseman (as well as Erol Tuzcu) will always sit with his back to the wall, even if he must sit in the rear of the room. Roy always wants to be able to see what is going on around him. Roy says,

> I cannot stand to be boxed in. I must have freedom of movement. I can't even stand to have my hand held by my wife or be restrained in any way. I am always on guard and get very uncomfortable if someone walks up behind me.

Dave Schoenian approaches every day always expecting an ambush. He is always on guard and constantly looking for an escape route. His home has a perimeter fence around it and, while he is still not completely comfortable, it does give him a limited sense of security. Dave avoids most places and situations where confrontations might occur. He does reconnaissance in everything he does, especially where he parks his car. He is always on guard, day and night. His dog is like a watch guard for him.

A walk in the woods is both comforting as well as challenging for Ray Shurling. Often he thinks, "This would make a perfect place for an ambush."

Booby traps were a constant reminder that one wrong step could cause death or at least severe wounds if we don't see the trip wire. It has become second nature for Bob Stumpf to always watch carefully where he steps. He is quite conscious of his surroundings. Bob walks his property with his dog and is very aware of securing his perimeter. He finds himself staring into the wood line and always fears he is in someone's rifle sight. On days he must go into New York City for a VA appointment or Vet Center group meeting, he takes different routes, and he travels when it is less crowded.

It is natural to us to scan spaces between automobiles in a parking lot watching for persons who might attack. We also at times will scan trees or the tops of buildings for possible snipers. At times, there seems no safe place, even to the point of avoiding open spaces. Some of us feel safe at night during sleep only if we have a weapon close to our bed. Sleeping under covers may be impossible because it restricts the ability to be "ready."

Again, for one who has never been exposed to combat trauma on a daily basis—where death was always possible behind every nippa palm, from any coconut tree, from any rice paddy berm, or from any stream bank—all of this hypervigilance may seem folly. However, when good buddies have died almost daily, it is not paranoia nor a phobia to have that heavily engrained sense of vigilance.

It seems impossible to unlearn that which earmarked our every waking moment while on combat operations.

STARTLE

"*Boo!*" For a child, the natural response is to jump or maybe even cry with fright when someone startles you. Our senses react as if we are suddenly jarred unexpectedly.

Every adult experiences reactions to sudden or loud noises. The combat trauma victim, though, will usually have very exaggerated reactions. The noises of explosions and even small-arms fire over and over have had a very lasting effect on us. The sound of a firecracker or the backfire of an automobile engine may sound exactly like an AK-47 being fired, and we may actually fall to the ground for "cover." To the unexposed, this may seem to be an extreme reaction. However, over and over, lives were spared by quick reactions in response to a blast. When this has happened hundreds of times, it stays with most of us for a lifetime.

Although he is able to absorb monumental levels of stress and turmoil with no trace of inward or external emotion, if someone walks up behind Tony Normand and he does not hear them coming, he gets weak, breathes rapidly, and lashes out angrily. Quick movements around Guy P. Moore can easily cause him to react in a very defensive and sometime offensive way. Fellow employees of Ray Shurling learned years ago to very carefully walk down the hall toward his office and make noises like humming or patting the walls so that he will know they are near. Recently,

Ray embarrassed himself in a restaurant with several friends and family members when the waitress approached their table from the rear and he reacted suddenly. Ray was aware immediately that his heart rate jumped markedly. He is embarrassed by his being startled, but nothing he does seems to ward off this type of reaction.

"Any loud noise or explosion scares the hell out of me," says Roy Moseman. "My heart rate goes up immediately and sometimes I will begin to sweat." Gunshots really get to Dave Schoenian. When he first got back from Vietnam, he went rabbit hunting with a friend. A bird suddenly flew up and Dave reacted and fired, just missing his friend. That was the last time he ever went hunting.

Once we are startled, the resulting arousal may be such that it takes an extended period of time to resume one's normal activities.

To us, a *"Boo!"* is more than a game. Rather, it instantaneously feels like life or death.

CONCENTRATION

A diseased heart can result in defibrillation where, instead of steadily pumping blood, the heart just flutters, which reduces proper blood flow to the body. This can result in passing out or death. Preoccupation resulting from the symptoms of combat trauma memories can cause mental defibrillation—a loss of concentration where many thoughts are trying to flow through one's mind simultaneously, with none effectively progressing. Repeated exposure to combat trauma has been proven to have a prolonged effect on concentration.

Roy Moseman has a very difficult time reading because after a page or two, his mind is off somewhere else. Often after reading three or four pages, he has no idea what he has read. "I have to really concentrate or be very interested in whatever I read. Also, I will be in a conversation with someone and the next thing I know I am thinking of something entirely different. That can be very embarrassing, but I can't seem to help it."

Prolonged thoughts of our combat trauma can also lead to loss of short-term memory. Dave Schoenian cannot retain a name, even after it has just been told to him. "Driving is becoming a hazard, my mind wanders, I forget where I am going, and I don't see what is going on in front of me. This frightens my wife to death."

Bob Stumpf says,

I have trouble remembering daily things like paying bills. I have lost or misplaced important papers and have let things lapse. I am preoccupied most of the time, find it very hard to focus or concentrate. My mind races. Sometimes it feels like it is going from frame to frame like a video of some sort. This behavior drives my wife up the wall.

Impatience and a short attention span interfere with Erol Tuzcu's ability to accomplish tasks that require concentration.

The operations officer for Ray Shurling's company is his son, David. "One single thought of Vietnam and you are done for the day, because you lose concentration, focus, and interest at work," David tells him. Ray also relates that recently, his CPA has found a number of accounting and bank statement errors, whereas in the past months these would pass with no mistakes.

Not only does the lack of concentration interfere with daily tasks and family relationships, it also from time to time has interfered with our efforts on the job.

⑬

GUILT, TRUST, DENIAL

GUILT

Right-thinking people feel guilty when things happen that cause regret, remorse, or sadness that the event(s) happened. In combat, these events happened almost daily. Four decades later, numerous events still ring in our minds that cause guilt, even when we may have had nothing to do with the event.

In addition to thinking he was dying after being blasted with those seven AK-47 rounds, in one of his more lucid moments while fighting for his life, Tony Normand remembers feeling searing guilt that if he died, his very young daughter would grow up with no father. "She would never remember me. I would be just a name and a sorry bastard who left her to grow up without a dad but with a wife who must carry the entire burden of raising a child as a single parent." Thankfully, Tony survived his wounds.

Months later, back in the States, Tony was part of a team detailed to inform a family that their son had been killed. As the terrible news was delivered and a semblance of composure was regained by the mother, she invited Tony to see her dead son's room.

When she opened the door and turned on the light, I felt a total weakness come over me. Tears came to my eyes and I could breathe only with difficulty. There on the wall in front of me, the face of her son was staring down from a very large framed photo. On my last night in the field prior to my injuries the following day, the *same kid* came to see me in the staging area. He was a brand-new replacement, small in stature and obviously very frightened of what tomorrow's operation would be like. He asked me if I thought God really looks after us, that he was scared and didn't know what to believe anymore. The first sergeant then came up and chewed out the new soldier for bothering me. I failed to see and understand the fright and loneliness of this young soldier, who feared he was going to die and needed someone to just listen and to reassure him that he would be OK. I failed to do the right thing. I erred when I focused on the big picture of the upcoming battle and my own preparation, but failed to care for the basic needs of one of my soldiers who would be in that battle. This omission is deeply embedded in my psyche.

Many of us had close calls when we normally would have been wounded or killed. This is especially difficult when others took our place and were killed or wounded, causing intense "survival guilt." John Adame was made a squad leader by his platoon leader. On the next operation, John was required to stay with the platoon leader. Suddenly, his squad was hit, and most of his men were lost.

We couldn't do anything to help them. I was really angry at myself for not being with them. They were all relatively new, but they were my men. I maybe could have seen something or done something to have saved us. But even if I had been killed, I was supposed to be there. Maybe I should have been one of those who died.

Company E 3/60th was flown into an area near Vinh Kim on the morning of April 7, 1968, and began making sweeping operations. Bob Stumpf was walking point but due to some allergic reaction, his eyes began swelling. The medic said it looked like hives and was probably a reaction to malaria pills. Bob was flown out on a resupply chopper for treatment.

Shortly after arriving at Dong Tam, our base camp, he began learning the awful facts of some events that happened minutes after he flew out.

At first I had no idea how bad it was. Leaving Vinh Kim, the VC had laid claymore mines in a bend in the road and set off a devastating ambush.

The first three men in the first squad and the first two men in the second squad were hit with the claymores, and the VC opened up and kept the rest of the company pinned down. They shot each of the five men in the head, and took all their weapons and a communications radio. They had no chance. I have agonized over this and continue to feel the guilt that five men were killed that day and one of them took my place. I do not know if I would have made a difference if I had been there. Maybe I would have seen something, but most likely my name would be on the Wall with them.

On June 19, 1968, Frank Martinolich's platoon leader, Lt. Oakes, was up front followed by the point man, Ron Honeycutt, Frank, and the platoon sergeant, Jon Winger.

Winger moved ahead of me just as the enemy opened up from a bunker directly in front of us, killing Lt. Oakes. Honeycutt was hit in the chest and had the charging handle shot off his M-16, which embedded in the inside of his elbow. As a result, he lost his arm. I waited to fire because I was not sure where Lt. Oakes was. Some of the other guys in the platoon yelled to me to open fire, that Lt. Oakes was probably dead. I then threw the grenades I had and took the ones Winger had and threw them too. Then one of our own gunships came in firing on our positions, thinking we were the VC. To this day, I only hope that the guy who told me to open up was right. I have spent my entire life wondering why I lived, why Winger stepped in front of me and took all those rounds, why the helicopter rocket did not kill me, and if I put any fatal rounds into Lt. Oakes.

Mitch Perdue, in remembering the fight mentioned in the previous section where Lt. Yount took over point, says, "If I had continued to walk point, Yount's bullet would have been for me. If I hadn't gone to the aid of our medic, Campbell's bullet would have also been for me." Mitch lives daily with his guilt.

Dave Schoenian remembers the day when God spared him.

I had just traded places with another soldier who wanted to fire the machine gun on the boat if we were ambushed. When the rockets hit the boat he took the blast in front of me; his leg was just about blown off and many others were wounded. Why him and not me?

Roy Moseman says, "I frequently think of all the good men who died in Nam and yet I made it home. I even think about the VC whom I killed, who had families and children just like we had." This all is a part of Roy's continuing guilt.

Someone has said, "The VC weren't human when I killed them. It was only later when they became human. Their death was the beginning of my guilt."

Guilt for Innocent Victims

Anytime the violence of combat occurs, innocent victims are very likely to eventually play a role in the soldier's massacred feelings when one is hurt or killed. Especially trying is when innocent children are caught in the crossfire of the insanity called war.

When innocent civilians are victims, and if it is our side that caused the carnage, guilt is almost sure to follow. Everyone can identify with children, and most of us saw children who were wounded or killed. Time does not always ease our guilt of knowing that children (and adults also) paid the supreme price of being at the wrong place at the wrong time.

I recall her as a little "rag doll." On the night of December 30, 1967, while I was with Company A, the adjoining company called in an artillery marking round. At daybreak the next morning, an old "papasan" (Vietnamese male) brought a small girl cuddled limply in his arms. She was wrapped in an old blanket, covered with blood. We saw that she had a massive head and face wound with her nose and part of one eye and cheek hanging grotesquely down almost to her chin. The casing from a part of the marking round had crashed through her little hooch as she slept and massacred her face. In looking at this small child then and even now, it is all I could or can do to keep from crying. I can still hear the gurgling in her little throat as she fought for breath.

The image of that broken and disfigured face is still very vivid to me. I don't even know if that once beautiful, black-headed child lived or not. At least we medevaced her, but even if she lived, she would have been disfigured for life.

Paradoxically, I have an adopted granddaughter (Maya) who is a very beautiful and loving jet-black-haired Mayan Indian child born in Guatemala. Maya Johnson and I have a very, very special relationship. Subconsciously and consciously, our interaction brings to mind that little black-haired "rag doll" child from four decades ago. The happiness that Maya provides for me helps to sooth the still-strong guilt of that other little black-haired, tan-skinned child who was mangled in a savage war.

Ray Shurling witnessed an incident in which a two-and-a-half-ton truck full of Vietnamese women returning to their village was leaving his compound. The driver lost control and the truck flipped, trapping many underneath.

> Some had limbs sticking from under the truck. It was at least forty-five minutes before we could get the truck turned over and get to the injured and dead. We used a Jeep, rope, and manpower to get the truck on one side. Limbs were severed. Blood puddled. At first there were screams and moans, but that went away as many of the women bled to death before we could save them.

It wasn't necessarily anyone's fault, but these women were just trying to make a meager living and it cost them dearly.

One evening at dusk, C/5/60th began taking incoming mortar rounds just as they were establishing their perimeter and settling in for some rest from the deep fatigue of walking tensely and alertly all day. The commander, Tony Normand, with the help of others located what appeared to be the source of the incoming mortars. He and two others moved into the open rice paddy to get a better line of where the mortars were coming from and to direct an air strike on the enemy positions. Taking small-arms fire, Tony and the other two moved back for better protection from the enemy fire just as the air strike came in on target. Immediately after the air strike, the enemy fire ceased.

Just before first light the next morning, Tony received a radio call from one of his outposts and said that three women and two children from a nearby village had come to their location and asked to see the commander. They wanted safe passage to look for their grandfather and a child.

> The women and children walked with me and a few of my troops to the location where the air strikes had hit the previous evening. They began wailing and crying as we came to a crater in the ground that was partially filled with debris and half a human torso, which they identified as that of

their grandfather. A few feet to the right was the bloody body of a young male child about eight or ten years old. We also found the base plate of a mortar and drag marks leading into the jungle, which were probably bodies of the VC who had fired the mortar at us.

It is a fact that as a result of my request to suppress incoming fire, these innocent lives were lost. Yes, my men were at risk. Yes, there was justification for me doing what I did. But I let myself down because I did not question a higher level of logic that put me in a war where I was at that time and ultimately led to the death of an old man and a child. I did a great job as a soldier and a lousy job as a man. All this is tough on my old brain.

A soldier threw a grenade into a bunker shortly after a firefight, believing some VC were in the bunker. When Roy Moseman looked into the bunker, he saw the heart-stopping sight of a little girl about three or four years old who had had her foot blown off. This poor little sobbing girl was vainly attempting to put her shrapnel-amputated foot back on her leg! Sad visions of that awful scene are often in Roy's dreams.

Flying into another of those wretched hot landing zones, Dave Schoenian was made the platoon sergeant for this operation. He had thirty green men. They were pinned down for hours. As a means of breaking out, Dave fired a light anti-tank weapon (LAW) into a nearby hooch. Then he fired at another person running in black PJs. Later, this person turned out to be a female "mamasan," and in the hooch were three dead kids. The contact with the enemy lasted for several hours. "You become so uncontrollable and take your revenge out on anything. I got so upset that I shot a water buffalo eighteen times and burned down several hooches."

Ray Shurling's compound was being mortared and nearby was a small child. Ray and the child were near the helicopter pad and not near cover. "I fell to the ground and pulled him under me. I curled up around him the best I could." Of course, Ray was terrified. But what about the kid? What about the thousands of other kids who probably to this day are haunted by the trauma of similar situations?

A buried mine exploded on the road from Dong Tam to My Tho. Five Vietnamese women who had been picked up at the MP gate were killed. Two of Bob Stumpf's buddies, John Hughes and Robert Ludwig, were with them and both were badly hurt. John had multiple wounds and lost an eye.

It is so easy now, four decades later, for someone who has never known the stresses of combat to judge the maimed and lost lives of innocent civilians. Our suffering is ongoing until we die, because the thoughts and feelings associated with the innocent never leave us.

Mistakes made during a combat operation can be costly to the innocent. It happens continuously in combat. Recently, Ray Shurling was digging in his attic for a map that he carried in Vietnam. He read the notes on the map that he made four decades ago. Like so many of us, Ray often wondered if there were times that innocent civilians were injured or killed by being at the wrong place at the wrong time when artillery was fired. No doubt there were many farmers, villagers, men, women, maybe children who were wounded or killed by being in those places we knew as "free fire zones." "Time and again I have asked God to forgive me. Maybe he has . . . but forgiving myself is another matter," says Ray.

The heavy load of knowing others suffered because of our decisions are often sources of guilt that many of us carry daily. Ray says, "It was 1969 . . . it was yesterday."

There were many times soldiers accumulated distress from being in combat for an extended period of time. This distress sometimes caused situations that later caused regret and guilt. In combat, there was little that could be done to relieve our distress or neutralize our guilt.

Our chain of physical and emotional wounds often places us in the category of feeling guilty when we see how badly our brothers had it who were dismembered and/or lost their lives. Our guilt often transformed into other feelings and became fuel sources for anger, sadness, and even fear that others would not understand—and they probably don't.

TRUST (OR LACK OF)

Returning from a year (or less) of a living hell where we saw so many of our brothers maimed and killed created a paradox of immense proportions in our souls. We went to Vietnam scared but curious and, for the most part, with a feeling that we were going to "fight for our country." Once it became clear that we were in reality fighting for our brothers beside us and that our country was on the other side of the world, without knowing it we began losing our trust.

Then, as we saw brothers go down, trust was eroded more and more, and our basic desire was to survive. It became very clear that our country would not save us; rather it would be our own ingenuity and trust in our brothers on either side of us that would save us. For some of us, even that wasn't possible.

Frank Martinolich decided very early on to "just trust myself and not get too close to anyone. As I was to find out too often, stupidity got more pronounced as the rank got higher. Some officers and sergeants didn't have a clue, so it was not wise to trust them." Frank goes on to say, "When it came to having to depend on someone else to stay awake when setting up ambushes or being alert, I trusted no one." This has carried over into Frank's life in that "I try to position myself to be able to have some control because I just don't trust much."

It seems safer to go by the dictum of "If you want it done right, do it yourself," because too many screwed-up operations got too many good brothers killed.

As mentioned earlier, during a firefight when Bob Stumpf was having brothers fall all around him, "Our new platoon leader was shooting at me with an M-79 from the rear because he had no idea where his men were positioned. That asshole caused me to worry about getting killed or wounded by an incompetent and candy-ass leader!!!!"

The erosion of our trust grew when strategic decisions of how this war should be fought resulted in the decision to "out–body count the enemy." What a way to keep score! Body counts became the only thing that mattered. "If I am killed, I will go on the scoreboard. Does my life not matter? Who other than the brothers in my unit and my family really care if I live or die?"

Most support troops had no idea what we were going through. When awards were put in for many of our brothers, often the paperwork was lost or misdirected. Yes, we know that the best award is to go home whole. But to be put in for a decoration and never receive it caused a tremendous loss of trust in many support troops who were "there to support us."

Mitch Perdue was put in for several awards but never received the award orders. John Iannucci was recommended for but never received several well-deserved awards.

John Adame was put in for a valor award. One of the support sergeants who never heard the sound of an enemy shot told John, "I'm going to see that it doesn't go through because you are a draftee." What an asshole. Of course, John did not receive the award.

A new lieutenant, Dennis McDougal, was shot in the chest by an enemy AK-47 in the city of My Tho at the beginning of Tet 1968. As he lay near death, bleeding from several parts of his body, a medic and I darted to him under fire and dragged him fifty yards to the relative safety of a hooch. Due to a paperwork backlog and so much constant combat during Tet, neither of us received the decoration for ourselves.

These thoughts of eroding trust mostly were buried deep down, but when we returned to the States, broken in mind, soul, and body, the loss of trust became more and more prominent. The hippies protesting in the streets were receiving all the attention. Our family and friends loved us, but so few knew our inner hurts and our disconnect from the brothers that we had left. The country at large didn't care about us at all. In many ways our country turned its back on us, both in Vietnam and after we returned. We went into combat as loyal citizens, but we felt abandoned. Even if they had known the hell we had been in, it was difficult to know if we could have trusted them or not.

Our young minds and decrepit souls were very confused and, in some ways, we are still very confused. We desperately wanted others to hear of our horror and trauma. But we were soon to learn that it was too great a risk to share experiences or feelings because others were not to be trusted with our feelings. One who has been exposed to repeat combat trauma does not and cannot talk about it like one would talk about the Super Bowl. Many of us feel that the only people we can really trust are other combat veterans. What a shame.

"I was mad at the world," says Terry Gander. And why not? Dave Schoenian has isolated himself to only having friends who are combat veterans. This gives him security. "I stay within my safe zone, which is my base camp. I am still in combat in my mind." Dave has worked very hard at the Pittsburgh VA by seeing a psychiatrist and attending group therapy every Thursday night at the local Vet Center. "Building trust in both places took some time, but now I can't go without the sessions. I'll do this the rest of my life."

Trust is a precious commodity for Ray Shurling. Even though he owns a multimillion-dollar company and has to depend on others to

make very important decisions, he still does not trust others. Being in
Special Forces, Ray did not have the support of an American squad in
that only he and one other American were together in a Vietnamese
unit. When setting up an ambush, the unit would split into two forces,
with Ray in one section and the other American in the other, leaving both alone with the Vietnamese soldiers, none of whom Ray ever
learned to totally trust.

Ray's unit always had a number of "Chieu Hois," who were former
enemy who had turned to the other side.

> I never trusted any of them. At any time they could have shot me dur-
> ing a firefight and no one would have ever known. Even in base camp, I
> always had a weapon ready in case one turned on me. To this day, I only
> trust three persons in my life: my son, who is my operations manager; my
> ex-wife; and my friend Jim Johnson, with whom I have entrusted many
> lifetime secrets, and he is a combat veteran.

When so much has happened to cause erosion of trust, many of
us have had an emotional bunker mentality when interacting with
others. We learned in the field that it is safer to have barriers of protection. Unfortunately, others have suffered by our emotional "hun-
kering down." But like an abused dog, we find it too risky to trust by
getting too close. To be exposed could very well cause us more pain
and suffering.

Relearning to trust is a huge mountain for many of us to climb. The
jagged edges of the cliffs and the deep crevices reinjure our exposed
nerve endings, and sometimes we must conclude that the effort to trust
is too great a challenge with so little possible reward. We admit that
making ourselves vulnerable and transparent by revealing our stories
of our life since Vietnam is a step of faith. Who can be trusted with the
details of our vile past? How can we not feel violated by their possible
disinterest, lack of understanding, or God forbid, their disrespect of our
emotions? Yet, it is our hope that if our stories are in any way helpful,
this is a step that we need and are willing to take.

Fortunately, some of us have learned to change "I can never trust
anyone about anything" to "I can trust some people some of the time
about some things."

DENIAL

From our earliest remembrances as a child, denial was a means of coping. If we "did wrong," denial might keep us from being punished. Denying we were sleepy might allow us to stay up longer. Denying to parents that we had homework might allow us to play outside longer. Sometimes, if we practiced our denial long enough and intensely enough, we came to believe our denial. Truth was obscured and a new "truth" became reality in our minds.

So it often is with the victims of combat trauma. Over the years, many of us have been in and stayed in denial that anything was "wrong" with us. We wanted to be normal in our thoughts and feelings so badly that we just buried our past experiences of combat and fought hard to keep them out of sight and out of mind. It just seemed so much easier to be in denial than to have to deal with the realities of our past. Unfortunately, all too often our denials would surface via nightmares, flashbacks, and intense feelings stimulated by seemingly benign events or situations

The fact is that exposure to combat radically changed us and damaged us internally in ways that are all but impossible to fathom. We males are taught to be macho and to suck it up when we are hurt or fearful. Behind our walls, we can create all sorts of illusions of reality pertaining to our histories. Occasionally, a combat vet whose behavior reflects his combat history is asked if he might need help. A typical response is an angry denial such as "I'm f------ fine. What's your problem?"

If a person has pains in their belly, fear that it might be cancer can cause a person to get into fatal denial. Everyone knows others who have neglected to seek help in diagnosing the source of their discomfort. So it is with the pain associated with our combat trauma. Actually, it has been only in recent years that Ray Shurling, Terry Gander, Guy P. Moore, Erol Tuzcu, Ron Miriello, and I have been able to begin dismantling our walls of denial and ask for and receive help from professionals. Our "later-life resurgence" of our historical combat trauma enabled us to get the help that we no doubt could have used years earlier.

Roy Moseman, Dave Schoenian, Bob Stumpf, John Adame, John Iannucci, Mitch Perdue, and Bob Nichols were able to remove their denial walls much earlier and get the help they deserved and needed. Good for them!

Even the government became very good at denial. Brothers who exhibited difficulties after combat "probably had something wrong with them before they went to Vietnam." It took years before there was any systematic recognition by our government that there was any such thing as PTSD. Agent Orange has killed thousands postwar. Yet, again, it took many years before the government acknowledged that Agent Orange was having the same effect as an enemy bullet.

It takes much courage and conquering of our fears to finally make the steps toward finding ways to help us with our historical trauma-associated emotional pains. We cannot find that courage, though, until we are willing to begin dismantling that dastardly condition of denial.

14

MEMORIES AND REEXPERIENCING COMBAT TRAUMA

Like computer popups that spontaneously appear on the screen, we have popups that suddenly appear in our mind's eye. They appear quickly and are almost always of a traumatic nature.

The Rung Sat Special Zone was known as the "Jungle of Death." It is impossible to imagine the dense combination of jungle and marsh, where at low tide there is knee-deep mud and at high tide, which can deviate as much as fourteen feet, we could be maneuvering in chest-deep water.

On September 7, 1967, B/3/60th and C/5/60th were beached in the leg-sucking mud. It took us over an hour to move two hundred meters inland. Without warning, the enemy hit us with small-arms fire, with bullets tearing through the foliage with terrifying sounds. Line of sight was only four to five feet in the heavy vegetation. Several were wounded near Guy P. Moore, Terry Gander, and me.

Soon, our artillery suppressed the enemy fire and they vacated a huge base camp, hospital, and supply depot. Rice was still cooking and many bloodstained rags and blood trails led away from their camp, indicating they had taken all their wounded with them.

As we moved out, there was another huge explosion. A booby-trapped 105mm round was tripped by Charles Hamilton, killing him instantly

and wounding three more. Charlie Taylor, the platoon leader, coura-
geously decided to walk point himself.

No grunt who ever maneuvered through that hellish place will ever
forget the misery that accompanied what seemed like the asshole of the
world.

Later, on a Road Runner operation, one of Charlie Taylor's APCs hit
a mine and was blown off the road into a rice paddy. One of his troops
had his foot and ankle caught in the track and road wheel.

> In order to keep him from drowning and to medevac him, right on the
> spot we had to amputate his foot above the ankle, cutting under water.
> Even though he was in shock, he cried in pain and kept calling for his
> mother. That tore my heart out because of the helplessness to do anything
> other than what was necessary to save his life. We could do nothing to
> save his foot.

A detonating wire to a booby-trapped grenade was found and Bob
Stumpf's new company commander, John Hoskins, decided to follow
the wire on his hands and knees. The unseen grenade went off in his
face, killing him. "It devastated all of us. I remember the results very
vividly."

A good friend of Bob's called Pop (Lonnie Tullier), who was in his
thirties, was on the way to R & R on August 12, 1968, when the chopper
taking him out crashed, killing Pop. "When I think of this, my thought
is that there was no justice in this f------ war." Then, on August 19, Bob
and his squad were called out to pull security around a downed chopper that had crashed. The carnage included four bodies burned beyond
recognition. Soon a recovery chopper landed. Bob vividly remembers a
young warrant officer down on his knees uncontrollably crying for his
burned buddies.

A few days later, Bob's unit was on a combat sweep of an area that
had been napalmed.

> We walked through what was left of a few hooches. In a small clearing
> were an adult person and a child burned to a crisp and both still in a
> standing position. A few moments later, my buddy, Joe Mangan and I saw
> a few gooks running from a hooch. We got off a few rounds and one of
> them went down. Joe saw some blood and we followed the trail. Under

some thatch, we found a dead boy. He was just a kid! I have carried these incidents for the past four decades and time does not make these memories any easier.

Running up and down Highway #4 at night with APCs to keep the roads open was pure folly to Tony Normand. "We were nothing more than opportunities for enemy soldiers to hone their marksmanship skills on a bunch of dumb American soldiers, who probably looked like a bunch of ducks crossing the stage in a shooting gallery."

The beginning of the infamous Tet offensive of February and March 1968 created horrible memories that remain with us like a Wild West gunslinger's six-shooter.

On February 2, 1968, the enemy was simultaneously attacking many major cities and base camps. Echo Company 3/60th Infantry was ordered to the city of My Tho. We left by boat during the night on a small stream and were ambushed in the dark, but orders were for us to run through the ambush firing onto the shore line with all our weapons, but not to stop and fight. We had one navy River Rat killed and several soldiers wounded, but we kept going. This was the beginning of weeks of constant combat.

The next afternoon, we arrived just outside My Tho, a city of seventy-five thousand. Prior to beaching, we saw heavy smoke rising from the city center, with fighter bombers making strafing runs at the enemy positions. John Adame describes it as

> being like a John Wayne movie with hordes of civilians streaming out with fear etched on each face and only a few personal possessions strapped to their backs. We soon established contact with the enemy, and we fought house to house. I went through three M-16s in four hours because each weapon would break. As it did, I'd get another weapon off one of our wounded.

We fought throughout the night and into the next day. Each hour brought more intensity into the battle. Enemy explosive devices had damaged and destroyed most structures. We moved past an orphanage that had been blown up. Rubble from the caved-in roofs had smashed the little beds of the children and their personal belongings were in disarray.

Heavy fire from the street in front of the orphanage became more intense, and we established a skirmish line just in front of the blown-up orphanage. Dennis McDougall, a new lieutenant, was firing an M-79 at the nearby VC when an AK-47 round plowed into his chest. As mentioned earlier, a medic and I ran to him, grabbed his unconscious and heavily bleeding body, and dragged him back to the edge of the skirmish line. Just then, a large shell slammed into our position, blowing up the hooch where we were caring for McDougall. Smoke and dust obliterated our vision temporarily and immediately we heard screams. Nine soldiers were wounded, with one having the lower part of his leg traumatically amputated in the blast. John Adame was in the adjoining hooch and was not wounded.

We evacuated the wounded and pushed forward. The enemy was now in full retreat and as we maneuvered down the main street, death and destruction were everywhere. Scores of dead bodies littered the street. Buildings and vehicles were blown up and many were in flames. Some bodies were without heads or limbs. It looked like King Kong had rampaged down the street and smashed everything in sight. A Vietnamese ambulance was extensively damaged, and the dead driver was crumpled down on what was the passenger side. We saw a pile of unexploded B-40 rockets the size of three bushel baskets, along with numerous AK-47s and Chi-Com carbines.

All the buildings had huge gaping holes and thousands of pockmarks from small-arms fire. A nearby small canal contained several bodies, including a baby floating face down. Next to the canal, a young Vietnamese mother was lying on her back, dead, with her head grotesquely twisted and her neck obviously broken. A whimpering infant lay on her body, attempting to nurse. A little farther down the street, a bicycle lay crumpled atop a prone young father whose fatal wounds were still oozing blood. Two hysterical children, a boy and a girl of perhaps three and five years old, were each tugging hard on the hands of their dead father futilely pleading with him to get up. Both children had cuts from shell fragments. As we continued to move, craters from explosions were everywhere, and storefront businesses were blown up like matchboxes stomped by a schoolyard bully.

As we were leaving the devastated city, an old gentleman offered us warm beer and soda and some peanuts in the shell. Most of us hadn't eaten since the day before. As we boarded our boats, little did we know that the memories of this hell would be etched on our minds for the rest of our lives.

I went into another hot landing zone with Echo Company, who were suddenly trapped in a V-shaped tree line just before dark on February 19, 1968. The VC were firing automatic weapons, small arms, RPGs, and mortars. Two helicopter gunships fired their rockets into our midst, thinking we were the enemy. During the night, we had seven brothers killed. By morning, the firing had stopped and the enemy had left. A resupply chopper came in and a medic, two other soldiers, and I loaded the seven mud- and blood-soaked bodies onto the chopper. Somewhere between the battle site and Dong Tam, one of the bodies, covered with slick mud and slime, apparently slid out the open door of the chopper unnoticed. The body was never recovered, and I frequently remember that family who not only lost a son but never had his body to bury.

The boat of Ron Miriello came to the aid of a Vietnamese unit. The VC "tax collectors" had butchered a village elder in front of the people to set an example of terror and control. He was still alive but both arms and both legs were cut off. He died soon after. Another time, a Vietnamese soldier had stepped on a claymore mine and had literally hundreds of holes in him. He was in shock with a blank stare on his face, but he had bled out and was soon to die. "I have viewed him hundreds of times throughout the years. It is the one that never deteriorates, never fades, and will never be lost."

Later, several boats were beached with diesel engines idling when Ron decided to cool off from the baking sun. He stripped to his underwear and dived into the muddy Mekong River, but before he could surface, the unexpectedly strong current forced him under his and several other gunboats with props running. His water safety instructor training saved his life. While under water, Ron vividly remembered the time as a kid when he fell into the Cape Fear River in North Carolina and was pulled to safety, unconscious.

Suddenly, the rice paddy was thick with enemy fire. The dike that Thomas Bright and Erol Tuzcu had for cover was only eight inches high. Bright was a new radio operator whom Erol was training.

We were a few hundred feet from the rest of the company. Bullets were cracking right above our heads. Bright began gurgling and almost immediately went motionless. A bullet had caught him near the neck-chest area. Even though I was lying right next to him, our shoulders touching, there was absolutely nothing I could do. He died before I even had a chance to call for a medic. I have *never* been able to get that gurgling sound out of my mind. Anytime I hear a similar sound, I feel as though someone has poured hot water over my head.

A large firefight in some rubber trees had the enemy all around Roy Moseman's squad.

We could hear them but couldn't see them. Another platoon took the brunt of the fight. When the fighting ended, my squad moved forward toward the other platoon. GI gear and weapons were lying on the ground everywhere, and at least a dozen dead soldiers littered the ground. One was lying on the ground with a claymore mine outstretched in his hand and he was holding the detonator in his other hand. It was obvious that when he was wounded, he decided he was not going to let the VC capture him. He was willing to blow himself up so that he wouldn't be captured. I can't imagine how frightened he must have been and what was going through his mind before he died. I continually see that dead soldier laying there holding that detonator.

The boat Roy was riding on was struck by a B-40 rocket on August 16, 1968, wounding him all over his body with many fragments, causing him to be hospitalized for six weeks. His right arm was severely injured when a piece of shrapnel about the size of a golf ball tore through his right bicep. "I can still picture the ball of fire and hear the explosion. It was like yesterday. I still smell the blood and see the explosion from the round." Often when Roy is driving, the memory of this or other trau-matic events pops into his mind—and suddenly he has no idea where he is going and sometimes where he is. It takes a minute to figure out what he is doing.

The night of August 12–13, 1968, was Dave Schoenian's first major battle. His platoon was overrun. The first position the VC hit had all the soldiers brutally killed. "I can still hear the screaming from that position of guys. The VC were all around us and I saw one gook throw a hand grenade at me as I shot him. The grenade landed on the other side of the dike I was behind."

The feelings associated with certain anniversaries of key events in our combat lives significantly impact us now four decades later. We all remember the date of arriving in country and the date we flew home.

Certainly, significant battles are at least annual reminders of events of life-changing magnitude. The Battle of Snoopy's Nose on September 15, 1967, is forever embedded in the mind of Terry Gander, who was wounded in that ambush. Charlie Taylor was not sure he'd even make it through the night. Guy P. Moore experienced the day because this was also his birthday and he thought that for sure September 15 would be his birth *and* death day. Tony Normand spent the night half submerged in the river for protection, when the river current floated a dead enemy soldier against his leg during the night.

I was the first to jump from the aid boat onto the well deck of a crippled boat moments after a B-40 rocket had exploded inside, killing two and wounding the entire platoon except for two soldiers. Seeing that huge pile of dead and wounded soldiers in the well deck is never far from my mind's eye.

Not a Thanksgiving Day goes by that John Adame and I do not remember the terrible tragedy of a booby-trap explosion that killed three of our brothers. The sister of one of the dead soldiers was actually engaged to another of the dead soldiers, whom she had met while they were in training in the United States. So this young woman lost both her hero brother and her fiancé in one horrible blast. Each year since, John has volunteered to work on Thanksgiving to help blot out the memories of that fateful day that nearly took his life as well. In conducting many Thanksgiving services over the years, I always find the reminders of that day cause me to be preoccupied with melancholy thoughts.

Leading a platoon of Vietnamese soldiers always had its challenges for Special Forces Sergeant Ray Shurling. Ray led his platoon into a deep valley to set up an ambush while a sister platoon set up for support if needed. Ray says,

Terrain was extremely difficult, but I get the ambush in place. I check claymore mines and wait. About 1:00 a.m. we hear them—VC moving in our direction just as I had planned. No one moves. We hear them talking as they get closer. The safety is off my CAR 15. I turn the radio off. We all are very tense. A few more yards and we will open up on the unsuspecting

VC. But they stop and come no closer. Damn, they have stopped to set up camp for the night. I pray that the far left of our platoon does not fire. The bad guys are not yet in place for an effective ambush. They can roll up our flank if we fire.

Hours pass. They have campfires, cook food, laugh, and talk. One VC even walks away from camp in my direction to take a piss. I see him clearly—so close I see the steam rising off his piss. I pray, "Please don't fire, please don't shoot this one. It's too early." We wait, and wait. Tension and fear is high in the quietness of the early morning darkness. The battle is near. They are going to walk right into our ambush when they move and it will be bloody. We are ready. Dawn begins to break and the VC stir awake. No one moves. But, it never happens. The VC pack up and move right back in the direction they came from. All is quiet and we move out.

This memory is never far removed from Ray's mind.

Later, as a vicious enemy attack on Ray's small Special Forces base camp occurred, a white phosphorus round fell short, landing unexploded on the runway of their airstrip. Being specially trained in munitions, it was Ray's responsibility to approach the round, bunker it with sandbags, and explode it in place. One faulty move could cause the round to explode and Ray's body would have been thoroughly cooked by the thousands of degrees of white phosphorus heat.

As mentioned earlier, Ray left for Vietnam with his best friend, Boyd K. Newbold. Ray saw Boyd hug his parents good-bye. Neither Ray nor his parents ever saw Boyd again, as he was killed in action. On his return flight from Vietnam, off-loaded first from the plane were fourteen coffins of dead soldiers. "I continually see these two images, one of Boyd hugging his parents and then those flag-draped coffins."

Being assigned as a radio operator at first was not what Bob Nichols wanted.

When I first arrived, my platoon sergeant, John Sperry, handed me the radio (PRC 25) and from then on I was a radio operator. For a long time I thought being a radio operator was a shit job, but later I realized that I always knew where we were, what was going on, where we were going, if the landing zone was hot or not, and a host of other information that the other riflemen didn't have. Unfortunately, what I remember the most was I was usually the first to know if someone was wounded or killed, and

I dreaded calling in the dust off choppers. Yet that was a part of my job that I always remember.

February 26–27, 1968, was a damning anniversary for John Iannucci, Guy P. Moore, Mitch Perdue, and John Adame, for this was the day that only twenty-six brothers walked out of the bush from that terrible battle that took so many lives.

When April 7 approaches, both John Adame and Bob Stumpf spend a difficult time attempting to deal with the losses they suffered that day in 1968. Dave Schoenian and Roy Moseman's worst anniversary date is August 12–13, 1968, when their platoon had seven of their brothers killed.

Memories can easily trigger those feelings that re-create scenarios which are permanently embedded on our souls. Remembering is not always a bad thing, though. Each of us has many positive memories. John Adame says, "I have some good memories such as certain music, the beer calls on the boats, of the heroes we left behind, listening to AFVN, and just getting a good break from the death in the field."

To remember both the positive and negative events can enable us to appreciate life now in ways that would not have been possible otherwise.

These are only a few of the memories that will never go away. We have thousands more, just like these. . . .

REEXPERIENCING OUR COMBAT TRAUMAS

Many of us have a daily dose of reexperiencing events that caused and still cause us pain, sadness, and horror. Our traumatic pasts are always only a cat's hair away, it seems. "When were you in Vietnam?" "Last night." It is always there.

A very pronounced event for all of us was 9/11, which caused us to want to lash out in anger, to hit something or scream. We felt helpless as in a firefight. The burning jet fuel and dead bodies created much rage.

The Virginia Tech massacre immediately sent a rush of intense feelings not unlike that which happened in a rice paddy or jungle canal during a firefight. Hatred, anger, fear, and disgust emerged when we saw the photo of the killer—an Asian face. This felt very much like the Asians in Vietnam who were our enemies.

At 9:00 p.m. on Christmas night 1975, I received a call from my beloved commander, boss and friend, Col. Swede Nelson, asking for help. He had been notified that his two sons, one nineteen and the other twenty-one, had just been in a horrible automobile accident, and he wanted me to meet him at the hospital. By the time we arrived, one son was dead and the other son and their two dates were horribly mangled. I spent the night at the hospital sitting and waiting with the family, not knowing if any of them would survive the night.

When I was leaving the hospital the next morning, a nurse asked me to take the clothing the sons were wearing and determine whether or not to give it to the family. The clothes were soaked in blood, broken glass, and body fluids. How many times had I helped a medic cut away blood-soaked clothing to determine the extent of wounds? This was combat all over again.

The entire surreal night was very similar to the feelings that I had experienced both with soldiers killed and wounded in combat as well as dealing with the grief of the next of kin. I conducted the dead son's funeral, traveled with Swede to northern Virginia to clean out the house of his dead son, and continued spending time with those remaining in hospitals—all the while fighting my own feelings that linked me to combat. It was months before I had quelled my feelings, but no one else ever knew the turmoil that was going on inside my soul.

Another horrible wreck occurred in 1976 just in front of me. A semitractor trailer hit an army truck, which then slammed into a civilian vehicle. Jumping from my car, I climbed into the overturned army vehicle, where a young soldier was trapped and the smell of gasoline was prominent. Calmly, I extracted the injured soldier through the broken windshield. Once safely back in my car, I fell apart, crying uncontrollably, for it was then that I realized that for those moments, I was in the middle of a firefight with a wounded soldier whose life had to be saved.

A U.S. postal worker in San Antonio was murdered in 1980. He had been shot five times and was brought into the emergency room at Brooke Army Medical Center while I was the on-call chaplain. Taking the sobbing family in to see the blood-covered body of their loved one was like being back at the Third Surgical Hospital in Dong Tam.

In 2004, I had a client who was a former Vietnam helicopter pilot. He had a heart transplant but his body gradually failed and he had an extended hospital stay. I was called to his bedside and I held his hand as he died. As I watched the color leave his face, I saw him, not as a fifty-eight-year-old heart patient, but rather as an army pilot in Vietnam who had just lost his life after having been shot down. I held my emotions in check for the family, but inside I was feeling ripped to shreds in fighting to control my memories from three and a half decades earlier, when I experienced so much death.

Barbara and I were traveling on the Amazon River in Brazil in 2005. We were with twenty-five other travelers who were being escorted into the jungle for a few hours. We were maneuvering on a small diesel-powered boat on a tributary, getting ready to disembark for the trek into the jungle. The stream was only a few meters wide, with overhanging foliage and the banks very heavy with mangrove and other heavy vegetation. I casually remarked to Barbara that it looked a lot like the Rung Sat Special Zone, aka the Jungle of Death, where we had several miserable firefights in 1967. With those words, I suddenly flashed back and was overcome with emotions of sadness and fear that included tears. I was embarrassed, but for those few moments, I was really back in combat in the Rung Sat, being inserted into that miserable jungle swamp.

It was 9:30 a.m. on December 23, 2006. All was normal in the Union Planters Bank in West Palm Beach, Florida. Erol Tuzcu had just entered the bank to make a deposit from his company.

All of a sudden there was shouting and that all-too-familiar shot from a pistol was fired. I turned around and there were three masked men, one with a shotgun and another with a pistol. 'All you mother f-----s, get on the floor right now!' The pistol-wielding robber started to pistol-whip the guard after taking the guard's weapon. The second robber stood guard at the door. I was the only customer in the bank, and the bank manager and I were spread-eagled on the floor with the third robber standing over us with a gun. As luck would have it, someone drove to the drive-up window and, unlike one of those regular bells that go off when a car drives up, it was an odd sound that these losers thought was an alarm. One of the robbers began shouting that someone had set off an alarm and to 'get the f--- out of here right now.'

During this ordeal all I could think about was how I was able to survive the inhumane conditions of Vietnam, the snipers, firefights, booby traps, et cetera. Now, I was sure I was going to get a bullet in the head. In an instant my thoughts were that after having survived that horrible ordeal, I was going to be wasted for no reason.

Talk about reexperiencing combat trauma. . . . I was shaking like a leaf and continued to do so for weeks. I struggled with my recurring nightmares, sleep deprivation, and other issues I was having. Even now, I have trouble even thinking about this renewed trauma.

During the monsoon season in the Mekong Delta, rain was a many-times-a-day event. To this day, Dave Schoenian is affected by rain and hot weather. He lives on a river and hears boats traveling periodically. When he drives down by the creeks, it reminds him of the streams we crossed many times and the Tango boats that took us on operation.

Only ten soldiers remained of twenty-one who began a combat operation for Dave Schoenian's platoon. After landing in a hot landing zone, they were trapped in a rice paddy for over a day, unable to move while the enemy picked them off, one by one. When they crawled out of the paddy, Dave left his backpack in the mud in order to more safely move under fire, and hopefully not be seen. After they reached the tree line, more were wounded from booby traps. Dave never retrieved his backpack. To this day, when seeing a backpack, he is immediately back in that horrible rice paddy under fire. "A part of me was left in that mud with my backpack."

In 2000, John Adame went to the Philippines on a World War II POW search. As he was returning from the search site, he passed through many rice paddies. He immediately became cold and clammy and felt exactly like he was returning from a combat operation. His very intense feelings lasted for several weeks.

When a dead soldier was returned from the field, the body was placed in a body bag to be transported to the graves registration in Saigon. Bob Stumpf spent his career in New York City. "The sight of garbage bags lying outside a building turns my blood cold. These images are reminders of so many body bags and send me back into combat and will probably never cease for me."

On July 15, 1968, Bob's unit did an eagle flight. After landing, another unit was being inserted by chopper when the landing zone became hot with enemy fire. The choppers did not land, but the door gunners opened up, apparently unaware of Bob's unit being in place. Four were wounded, including Tommy Lynn who was hit in the head, but still breathing. Bob, Jim Toney, and Sgt. Bruce carried him to a dustoff, but Tommy soon died. In May 2000, Bob received a call about Tommy.

> I was caught completely off guard. It brought me right back to that time. I literally started shaking at my desk. I had to leave work and walked around for hours. The inquiry was from Tommy's brother, James. We later met at the Wall and Jim Toney and I, the last two to see Tommy alive, were able to interact with his brother.

Just after dark on another combat operation, Sgt. Paul Fusco was walking out to check on his squad's position. He must have gotten turned around because he walked right in front of his M-60 machine gun position. He was hit so many times you couldn't even tell it was him. Bob and two other soldiers wrapped his body in a poncho and carried it some distance to where it could be picked up by a chopper. "I had blood and gore all over my fatigues and boots. I can still see and smell this and can still hear the sloshing of his blood inside the poncho."

It is strange how things come full circle. Bob says,

> A friend sent me a book entitled *And a Hard Rain Fell*, by John Ketwig. Paul Fusco was Ketwig's best friend in high school, and his name in the book caught me completely off guard. I recently visited the Rochester, New York, Vietnam Memorial and found Paul's plaque. I broke down and cried for Paul Fusco and his family. It took almost forty years for these feelings to come out!

Memorial services always cause Roy Moseman to reexperience his combat trauma. In Vietnam, for a while, every time they came in from an operation, there was a memorial service because so many of his brothers were being killed. It was a memorial, yes, but it was a continual reminder of brothers who had just lost their lives. Now, Roy attends memorial services out of respect, but they always cause him to reexperience his trauma.

Both Roy and Bob Nichols have sons who are career soldiers. When their sons were ordered to Iraq on several deployments, both Roy and

Bob went through so many emotions that resonate with their times of combat trauma four decades prior. Bob says, "His deployment has caused me a lot of pain and grief. I am suddenly slam-dunked with the reality of the horrors of combat. Not only am I worried to death about his safety, I am seeing all the crap again in my mind that I experienced forty years ago."

Like in a flashback, so many events can cause any of us to suddenly be back in a terrible firefight, helping a wounded brother, covering a dead brother, or lying in sucking mud with bullets and explosions all around. Like Ray Shurling said, "It is now, but it is 1969."

Yes, some of us reexperience combat almost on a daily basis.

⑮

WORK AND CAREER

After the trauma of combat, we returned to the States and tried to pick up a new life. Some of us had families already and the rest of us soon were married and had children. Therefore, developing a career in order to make a living to support our dependents was soon a pressing concern. Unfortunately, combat does not train one for the civilian workplace. In fact, it often is an impediment to productive work.

All of us eventually developed careers and have worked the majority of our adult lives, albeit often with the feeling that we were still fighting different kinds of battles. All of us have been handicapped to a degree due to lingering effects of our combat trauma.

Initially, several of us struggled. Dave Schoenian was in neutral for a year before working for a power company for over thirty years. Roy Moseman also floundered but eventually opened his own thriving electrical contracting business. Guy P. Moore was somewhat lost in himself but eventually had a very successful career with Ford.

Erol Tuzcu had emigrated from Turkey, having a keen desire to have a better life in America. After Vietnam, he failed at two business ventures due to his drinking and two failed marriages. Then he developed a very successful manufacturing business making wood floors and roof trusses. Now, many years later, he is living his dream, albeit with much hard work, with fourteen-hour days and working some on all weekends and holidays.

Ron Miriello became a community college vice president. After working for Western Publishing for a number of years, Ray Shurling established his own business, Cape Fear Distribution, Inc., a warehouse and storage facility. Bob Nichols was very fortunate in that he drew only one unemployment check and then went to work for a power company. He worked for thirty-three years and retired at age fifty-five. Charlie Taylor became a financial planner and manages in excess of a hundred million dollars. Bob Stumpf was a successful banker in New York. Mitch Perdue was a purchasing manager in the lumber business. I had a career in the army and earned four degrees, becoming a marriage and family therapist as a second career.

Working very long hours each day was a way that John Iannucci tried to suppress the many associated feelings from his combat trauma. Fortunately, after a few years, John took the large step of opening his own Italian restaurant in Ashville, North Carolina. His very hard work and long hours for more than three decades turned his restaurant into a very popular eating establishment, and his business continues to boom.

After nine of us had successful careers, later in life we had to cease working due to exacerbation of our PTSD symptoms. These include Roy Moseman, Dave Schoenian, Guy P. Moore, Terry Gander, John Adame, Mitch Perdue, Bob Stumpf, Terry Gander, and me. More about this later in the chapter.

Two of us stayed in the army, including Tony Normand. Despite his terrible wounds, which involved losing a kidney, Tony fought to remain on active duty. He literally became a workaholic, which took him to the top as he retired after thirty years. His last job was chief of staff for the army's Special Operations Command at Fort Bragg. Upon retirement, Tony did not miss a beat and took a position in a nearby county to develop and attract industry. Many weeks, Tony still works seventy to ninety hours per week.

John Adame worked for the Postal Service. He was known as a Vietnam vet, and a part of his demeanor caused other workers to know not to push him too far. There was fear that he could "go postal," in that numerous violent actions have occurred in the Postal Service when a worker was pushed too far. When John was fifty-six, he knew that if he didn't leave, he easily could "do something bad." Rather than losing a pension, benefits, and maybe going to jail if he "went over the edge," John retired.

Thirty-two years on the same job for Frank Martinolich proved beneficial for him and others.

> I questioned management on everything, and just like in Vietnam we had a great deal of incompetence in management. Stupid and bad decisions in Vietnam put our lives on the line, and here the same stupidity put our livelihood on the line. I became a union shop steward to be able to represent myself and others from being unjustly wronged. It was a license to argue or discuss issues. I became very good at it.

Statistics indicate that an inordinate number of veterans are street people. We cannot pass judgment on the reasons some sleep under bridges, eat from trash cans, or camp out permanently in the woods. We can say that, but by the grace of God, there could go any of us. Yes, we worked hard and supported our families. Some of us now get financial assistance from the government due to our disabilities. All of us paid a price from combat that has made our jobs and careers more complex and the struggles to maintain our emotional stability a challenge.

GO TILL YOU BLOW

Several decades ago, when stock car racing was gaining popularity in the southeastern part of the United States, there emerged basically two types of race car drivers. One was the driver who saved his car until near the end of the race and who went just fast enough to still be in the race near the end. That driver had the theory that "I cannot win if I blow my engine early in the race." The other type of driver would keep the "pedal to the metal" and run his race car as fast as he could. If he blew up his engine, then it blew up. A common saying about such a driver was that he'd "go till you blow."

This has been not too unlike some of us who have lived our lives with the symptoms of combat trauma. We fought the symptoms for as long as we could and eventually some of us simply blew our emotional engines and had to go the garage, out of the race. In attempting to suppress the massacred feelings that many of us carried, working extremely hard and long hours, along with denying the dangers of untreated or un-dealt-with combat trauma has caused several of us to "blow," ending our career.

The symptoms of PTSD caused deep depression for Terry Gander, and he had no choice but to retire early. His trauma symptoms became severe enough that he was hospitalized for awhile.

Likewise, John Adame had worked for the U.S. Postal Service for many years. John realized that he could easily get out of control if pushed too hard. He didn't want anything bad to happen and had no choice but to retire early.

The only productive work Guy P. Moore could find when he returned from Vietnam was in an auto plant. Many years on a career progression that began to reverse itself brought back many bad feelings of combat for Guy.

> The company decided to eliminate my job and put me back on a job I had twenty years prior, on the assembly line. I had to retire because my mental health could not deal with the rejection and demotion. I had no other skills or hobbies. I got depressed and it was almost unbearable. I had a lot of anxiety, irritable mood swings, homicidal and suicidal thoughts, high blood pressure, severe headaches, stomach problems, as well as a resurrection of survivor guilt from Vietnam. I don't really know why, but I kept having thoughts of my combat times. I had horrible feelings that I was going over the edge, and no sense of future. I didn't care much about anything, especially myself.

It was soon after "blowing" that Guy went into inpatient treatment for PTSD at the North Chicago VA Medical Center.

Roy Moseman actually blew twice. After leaving the army, Roy worked in a plumbing and electric supply company warehouse, then did inside and outside sales, became an estimator, then vice president of his company—and then he blew. He had an argument with the CEO and literally walked out the door. He began his own business, Classic Electrical Contractors, a commercial and industrial electrical construction company. "In 2004, my PTSD symptoms had gotten much worse and I was no longer mentally able to take the pressure involved in my work. My private and VA psychiatrists told me I needed to get out of the pressure and problems on me." Again, Roy immediately blew.

> I think so many people, including family and friends, do not think there is any such a thing as PTSD. Most think it is just a way to get money out

of the government. I closed a multimillion-dollar business because of my combat trauma symptoms. I could have made one hell of a lot more money in my business than I am drawing from disability.

The lumber business was what Mitch Perdue knew very well. He lived and worked in various parts of the country. Having a boss who was also a Vietnam veteran enabled Mitch an outlet to talk almost daily about the effects of his combat trauma. They became very close. Suddenly, the boss was promoted and left. Mitch lasted only six more weeks. His support had left. He left good money and benefits, all because he blew.

Work became the enemy for Dave Schoenian. Sometimes he would even see "enemy" faces on the people near him at work. He became constantly on edge and was always ready to fight if there was any sort of confrontation. For years Dave had cleverly disguised his mental situation and kept on a smiling face; all the while the symptoms of his PTSD were eating him alive. Having worked for thirty-three years at his power company, he was called out for a problem in the plant one night.

> I was having severe trouble concentrating and safety was an immediate issue. I called a friend, who came to the plant to help me with the problem. I knew then I was mentally done. I was scared to make a mistake. When morning came, I told my boss, "I am going home; the war here is over for me." I never went back.

After Dave blew, realizing the severity of his condition, his wonderful wife, Ella, told him, "Honey, we'll eat peanut butter every day if we have to." This affirmation made him go to the VA for the first time and get help with therapy and medications. The VA also awarded him a 100 percent disability rating for his PTSD, and fortunately Social Security disability also came through for him.

Several emotional explosions contributed to Bob Stumpf's blowing. Working in New York City as a vice president for the Israeli Discount Bank, Bob had very high distress in his job. The most prominent was the morning of September 11, 2001. Bob was at work when the World Trade Center towers were hit.

> I went outside (Fifth Avenue) and saw the second jet hit. I saw the huge fireball that carried through from one side of the building to the other. By the time the first tower came down, people who were close to the towers

were working their way uptown. Looking downtown all you could see was a tremendous cloud of dust.

The next day I came back into the city and worked most of the day. About 10:00 a.m. there was a bomb scare in Grand Central Station and the Pan Am building, which caused a massive evacuation. The panic was unbelievable. I saw one woman actually run out of her shoes. The streets and sidewalks were jam-packed with hysterical people.

Thereafter, I was hanging on by my fingertips. I became depressed, my anxiety level increased, and I could not sleep. I was having more trouble getting along with people at work. Nowhere seemed safe for me. I could not relax, had extreme hypervigilance—much anxiety and a feeling of dread were always with me. All of these factors were now ratcheted up to the nth degree.

So, Bob Stumpf also blew. Continuing to work became impossible for Bob. Soon after ending his career, he was sent to the Batavia, New York, VA Medical Center for a month of inpatient PTSD treatment.

After going back to school to get my doctoral degree in marriage and family, I had fully intended to work into my seventies. I loved my job as a therapist, was very good at it, and had a tremendous reputation of therapeutically helping people. However, gradually I began experiencing increasing flashbacks, nightmares, and extraordinary fatigue, causing me to vegetate on the sofa after work. I did not want to talk on the phone and found it more and more difficult to concentrate. I had been and continued to be a very outgoing, humorous, and vivacious personality who had countless friends. Yet, few knew what was really going on inside of me. Like Dave Schoenian and most of the others, I had a public facade that masked the inner trauma and terror from four decades earlier that continued to eat out my insides.

Several events occurred that clearly showed that my emotional engine was blowing. One of the most marked was leading a training session for staff when suddenly, while referring to a decision that probably saved my life in Vietnam, without warning I was overcome with emotions resulting in sobbing and beating the table with my fists. This was the final straw, so to speak, that made me realize I could no longer function professionally, and I made the very unpleasant decision to end my career.

Although our stories are not intended to be clinical in nature, it may be of interest to see an example of how combat traumas can devastate a person years later. Following are some clinical excerpts of a PTSD assessment by Dr. Tomi MacDonaugh of the Fayetteville, North Carolina, Vet Center on my problems that caused me to blow.

March 2, 2005—James D. Johnson

A. Overview of Progression of PTSD Severe Reactions

Onset: He began to psychologically deteriorate in May–June 2004 due to PTSD reactions. This alarmed him so much that he entered into mental health counseling at the local VA Medical Center. His vocational goal was to keep working indefinitely. But his self-assessment was, "I started to spiral down." He reduced his work load to ¾ of his usual work, hoping this would enable him to remain working for some time.

Emotional collapse: He planned and conducted various team-building and personal self-exploration exercises for the church staff of eleven. To his shock, during one of his sessions, he began recalling traumatic events in Vietnam that suddenly created emotional turmoil. After 5–6 minutes while recalling how his life had been saved during combat, he was immediately emotionally overwhelmed to the point that he had an emotional catharsis and began beating the table with his fists. The staff was shocked. He was extremely embarrassed since "I did not see it coming," and he concluded, "I blew it" (failed to perform adequately). His basic assessment was "I became unglued in public," and he left hurt, embarrassed, and feeling guilty.

Resigning as a pastoral counselor: After fifteen years of pastoral counseling, his options and decision making were reviewed today. It is clear to me that he was emotionally exhausted and overwhelmed to the degree that he needs to stop working as a therapist and focus on treatment (mental health) for himself on a long-term basis.

B. PTSD Symptoms Assessment

Criteria A for PTSD: He previously reported a total of 28 types of combat traumas in Vietnam in an intake assessment here by me on 12-23-03.

Criteria B for PTSD: With regard to persistently experiencing traumas, in working with family members of a deployed soldier, he became very emotionally involved, cried, and it intensified his own feelings about past war trauma. He has repeated combat-related nightmares which are very vivid and distressful.

Criteria C for PTSD: With regard to persistent avoidance of traumatic cues and numbing of responsiveness, he realizes he was making attempts to avoid dealing with Vietnam—but the intense emotions were "breaking through" so to speak. He has a marked diminished interest in previously enjoyed or meaningful activities. Although he wrote three PTSD articles for publication, his draft for a second book from a victim/provider point of view overwhelmed him and he decided he could not do it.

His restricted affect was predominately despondency. Although he stopped writing, he could not stop the intensification of his feelings. His emotional extended outburst at the staff training that he led was the culmination of the emotional process due to unresolved war traumas.

Criteria D for PTSD: The cathartic release at the staff training involved the release of intense anger and rage, which had been stored up for years. He had an "all-or-nothing" reaction, which is typical of severely impaired PTSD cases. His concentration difficulties now result from the blatant emotional turmoil which is unresolved.

Criteria E for PTSD: The duration of the clusters of PTSD symptoms is clearly chronic, still persisting since leaving Vietnam on June 23, 1968. His PTSD symptoms are intense and severe in degree.

Criteria F for PTSD: He is severely impaired and distressed in several functional areas to the point he is totally unemployable on a long-term basis due to chronic and severe PTSD.

His mood is clearly disturbed with intense feelings of despondency, which are clinically obvious, but with apparent suppressed anger and rage.

Typical of dynamic, high achievers, LTC Johnson (Ret) was able to perform well as a pastoral counselor over 15 years despite underlying PTSD problems. But the "Go until you blow" dynamic finally occurred with his ending up totally unemployable.

LTC Johnson now is so severely impaired due to chronic and severe PTSD that he requires long-term psychotherapy on an individual and/or group basis with other combat veterans with PTSD.

Like Guy P. Moore, Frank Martinolich and Bob Stumpf, I was referred to a month of inpatient PTSD treatment at the Batavia, New York, VA Medical Center.

None of us who have blown are happy about it or even profess to understand it. Our views once were, "If I can survive combat, I can survive anything." In many ways, we have. However, the lingering effects of repeated combat trauma got to us, and while we once were perhaps ashamed that we blew, we now try to accept the reality of the emotional impact of what happened to us. In many ways it is still happening to us.

16

FAMILY, FAITH, AND MORALITY

FAMILY

The ideal for family members in any culture is to nurture, care for, and love other family members. One depends on this love to enhance the good times and to transcend the bad times. For us who have been traumatized in combat, we have had a variety of influences from family. Unfortunately, most of those close to us do not really know what we experienced; not that they do not care, but rather that all too often we have become protective of our feelings. Often we have been very reluctant to reveal our feelings or details of our past, out of fear of not being understood or even of being rejected. Plus, if they really knew what happened to us, the risk is great that just by knowing, they could be emotionally injured as well. How could another person understand, when more often than not *we* do not understand? We just know the feelings are there.

All of us have some regret at how we have treated our loved ones. Some of our parents, wives, and children have been negatively affected by our behaviors resulting from our traumatized souls. The emotional infection from our combat trauma has transcended ten thousand miles and extended to other generations, who became recipients of our "wounded souls." Neglect and even abuse of our loved ones have occurred on occasion. Our confession is that just because we were abused in combat in no way is an excuse to mistreat anyone, much less our loved ones.

Many traumatized combat victims go through multiple relationships because of inability to control our feelings, angry and unreasonable outbursts, melancholy behaviors, and an overall reluctance to let a loved one get close. As a result, relationships often deteriorate, and separation may occur because "I no longer know who he is" or "She can't relate to me and my past." Domestic violence frequently occurs within traumatized families.

Terry Gander says, "When our children were young, I kept the effects of my trauma hidden from them. I didn't want them to be affected by it." Ron Miriello says, "My trauma has indeed affected my wife. However, she is not even aware that I deal with PTSD. It's the way I choose it to be. My children have also been affected by it by my occasional display of unexplained anger."

Barbara Iannucci is a queen of magnificent proportions in that she almost single-handedly gave John reason to live after his return from Vietnam. John says,

I married my high school sweetheart in 1971 and without her support, it would have been hard to convince me that life was worth living during those early years. She and my three sons are the reason I get up every day and the reason I now look to the future with a sense of joy and anticipation. They became the glue that held me together.

Before Vietnam, John Adame was happy and outgoing.

After Vietnam, I fell in love with Maria and we got married. Unintentionally, I put her through hell. I did some bad things to her. I drank a lot to numb my pain and I wouldn't talk to her. I didn't feel she nor anyone else could understand. I also treated my daughters unfairly. I was withdrawn from them. I was there, but not there. I refused to get involved. They kept their distance to protect me, I guess. Or maybe it was to protect themselves.

Maria's hell, though, did not really get going strong until I stopped drinking. At that point, my PTSD really kicked in and Maria's life was miserable because of my lingering combat trauma. I'm sorry it was that way but finally we have discussed our relationship. I had been close to family, but again, after Vietnam, I was withdrawn. When I would attend family gatherings, I would just sit off to myself. I'm finally getting back with the family now after all these years.

Guy P. Moore says, "I have many times made life a living hell for my wife and daughter." Yet, Joann has been a steady force of commitment throughout the hard times with Guy.

Being a Turkish immigrant, Erol Tuzcu was married and divorced twice before he married Susan almost three decades ago.

> Susan is behind me all the way for better or worse, til death do us part. Even though I am not very verbal about my feelings, she is always attentive if I do feel a need to express myself. Other family and friends don't really understand about my trauma because they didn't see or hear or feel what we did. Earlier, my children called me a grouchy old fart.

Ella Schoenian has been an unwavering force in Dave Schoenian's life. "Over the years I have put Ella through pure hell, being a total asshole, drinking, carrying on, and keeping to myself." When Dave went through such difficult times at work while fighting the never-ending effects of his trauma, Ella encouraged him to leave work. Ella knew that Dave was fighting still another battle at work. Her loving support has gotten Dave through so many very difficult times. Ella believes she, too, now has PTSD as a result of how Dave has unintentionally treated her. Fortunately, Ella now goes to most of the treatments with Dave.

Other than his psychologist, Roy Moseman says his wife, Lynne, is the only one who understands his past trauma and the only one who cares.

> Lynne has put up with more from me than I would have ever put up with. She has taken the mood swings, the verbal abuse, the anger, the depression, and everything else. It has been very hard on her and I love her so much for trying to understand what I have and am going through.

Several of us have had multiple marriages and relationships. Frank Martinolich says,

> It usually comes down to not being able to share myself the way I am expected to. I'll only let them in just so far, but not enough to make myself feel vulnerable. Because I know my underlying anger is so strong, I usually will shut down and not want to get into an argument, which leads to a deterioration of the relationship. Then, I don't have any emotional attachment once the relationship is gone. It's just like dealing with things in Vietnam—deal with it at the moment, be satisfied, and move on.

Interestingly, the first of Frank's three marriages produced two sons, and he was an effective single parent to them for eleven years.

Intergenerational combat trauma symptoms occurred with Mitch Perdue, in that his father was a World War II veteran who heroically guarded a key bridge for the Allies against the Germans as they attacked. This bridge was the only bridge in the region left standing.

After the war, Mr. Perdue began working for the railroad and shortly became a foreman with a bright future. However, he continued to have problems associated with his combat and began drinking heavily. He lost his job, his family turned against him, and in desperation, he went to a local bridge and committed suicide. Mr. Perdue left a wife, two young daughters, and Mitch, who was only five years old at the time.

Recently, Mitch found a letter dated July 12, 1952, by George R. Blalock, MD, that was written shortly after the suicide. It states:

> I have known the late William Perdue, Jr., since he was a small boy and, being the family physician, have had occasion to see him on many visits to the home as he was growing up. Before he became a member of the US Army, he seemed a perfectly normal person in every way. Since his return from the Army, I have noted that he seemed a different person. He was more irritable, nervous, quiet, and did not care to mix with people. He had something on his mind all the time. . . . His wife tried to get him to consult a doctor, but he never would do so. The change in his personality was gradual but definite . . . with a marked change. From my observation, this change in personality was a definite result of some condition during the time he was in combat.

Clearly, Mitch's father suffered the same symptom from WWII combat that many others in succeeding periods of combat have. Dr. Blalock just didn't have a name for the condition then, but we know now it was obviously untreated PTSD that led to the suicide.

Mitch has lived with the results of the terrible history ever since. As a means of trying to come to terms with his father's suicide and his own combat trauma, in 1988, Mitch, his wife Debbie, and their two daughters flew to Germany and visited the very bridge that had been guarded by his father.

Debbie Perdue describes her plight with Mitch as follows:

Mitchell gets mad at his family over trivial things and cannot seem to put things into perspective. He has nothing to do with his in-laws and has had actual fist fights with his father-in-law. He has not participated in our children's activities at school. We have been through many trying times in our four decades of marriage—two miscarriages, health problems and illnesses, job instabilities, deaths, etc. But, I will be there for him until he dies, God willing.

Ray Shurling believes, "In hindsight, my combat trauma may have caused my divorce. My anger, drinking, sadness, and withdrawal certainly contributed to my divorce after sixteen years." Ironically, though, Ray says that Debbie, his ex-wife, is one of only three persons he totally trusts today.

Having a wife as one's best friend and confidant, like Diana is to Charlie Taylor and Barbara is to me, has made our lives very much more pleasant. Even though they weren't there, their compassion has been a gift from God to Charlie and me. There is no substitute for having a loved one listen to the details of difficult experiences.

Bob Stumpf says it best:

I continue to have and will always have problems in day-to-day life. No person, especially our families who have stood by us and suffered along with us, should live with this kind of pain and burden, but the reality is that we do. My wife, Mary, has been the rock of our relationship. She has kept us strong all these years, has stood by me through it all, and her love and devotion to me, our children and grandchildren never wanes. I draw on her strength and courage every day.

Family members who become secondhand victims of our trauma suffer distress often as intense as the returning vet experienced. How we are impacted in later years after our trauma depends to a large degree on our pre-trauma experiences such as childhood upbringing, values, and nurture and affirmation as a child. Without support early in life and current support from loved ones, a higher risk exists for experiencing ongoing PTSD.

We are grateful for those who loved us and for their commitment to support us "for better or worse," while not understanding what was going on with us but knowing there were demons inside us from our Vietnam past. Even when we made it worse, most of our loved ones stuck it out with us. And we thank you from the bottom of our hearts!

FAITH AND MORALITY

"O God, help me!" is more than a trite statement made in a momentary state of acute need. In the midst of an ambush when all hell has broken loose and one cannot think because the noise of explosions and gunfire is tearing one's nerve fibers to shreds, asking for God's help may be the only utterance one can make.

Our stories are not theological discussions of "Where is God in the midst of combat?" While certainly important, that concept is beyond the scope and intent of our stories. However, our call for God's help is made more realistic when one later looks back and deals with the status of his own faith in the midst of chaos and soul-searing fear. Some of us feel soiled because of some of the things we did. We even ask, "How could God have let these terrible things happen? Is it God's intent for me to suffer like this? When is enough enough?"

"There are no atheists in foxholes" is more than a cute line from a co-median. When life seems ready to end and a troop is thousands of miles from home and the exploding, out-of-control environment is far more than his young brain can comprehend, panic faith becomes very real. Later, we may even question God. Guy P. Moore says the God he once knew died in the battle at Can Tho on February 26–27, 1968, when his company was wiped out except for twenty-six men. "To this day I still have trouble getting close to God."

Seeing brothers wounded and killed actually deepened Charlie Taylor's faith in God. "When in combat, I could feel God's presence. I firmly believe that my faith in God helped me then and now. Upon my return home, those in my community of faith were very supportive of me and of what I had done."

Not meaning for it to be just a metaphor, Tony Normand says, "One thing I did learn from my being shot seven times is that angels do not necessarily need great white wings to help us out. They can also fly about in big, green helicopters. The angel who saved me went on to become a two-star general."

On the first Sunday in Vietnam, Ray Shurling went to chapel. He then was assigned to a Special Forces A-Team and only saw a chaplain once after that. "He flew in to our compound for about an hour. I can only remember that he had on spit-shined boots—in the jungle."

Needing and asking for forgiveness is an ongoing issue with Ray. After an encounter with the enemy where some events were left in question regarding such things as "free fire zones" and exactly who is the enemy, questions of right and wrong haunted Ray—then and now. "Time and time again I ask God to forgive me. Maybe he has, but forgiving myself is another matter." Ray's faith played a huge role for him during his entire tour. "I always believed that God was going to take care of me and protect me. I had great faith that God would get me home, and to this day I believe He did. I wore a cross taped to my dog tags. I frequently held it and prayed for God to protect me."

We had to put moral dilemmas of killing and maiming on hold. Our choice was to kill or be killed. The task was to stay alive because to get killed meant that nothing else mattered. Morality had to wait until later to be figured out. To some of us, it has taken a lifetime. John Adame says,

> I read somewhere that when one is in combat, his soul dies but the body lives. We become walking bodies with no real spirit inside. I see myself as one of those walking bodies. My spirit died in Vietnam, as I had all the moral teaching of my childhood severely damaged. I had been taught that human life is something we must respect. In Vietnam I learned that human life is to be killed if it gets in your way. The ones who died were probably the lucky ones. They went to heaven and we who made it home must live in hell for the rest of our days.

Ron Miriello avoids being seated in places where people are at his back. However, in church, "God grants me complete comfort in His house even when seated in the front and this amazes me." Ron also says, "My abilities to deal with my combat trauma are simply gifts from God. It is only through the grace of God that I remain strong emotionally."

This is how Roy Moseman sees it:

> I am not a real religious person, but I find myself asking God for help and understanding on many occasions. I have begged him to help me during my worst times. I may be a hypocrite because I am not in church every Sunday, but I know He is with me when I call on him.

Dave Schoenian says,

> The Lord has guided me my whole life. I have not done right by attending church much, but for some reasons God has helped me and my family. We all have hardships, but you must have faith to get you through.

Our spouse's faith is also what helps them deal with us. Debbie Perdue says, "I have put my faith in God, who has helped us through so many difficult times and circumstances."

Probably all of us at one time or another, when feeling overwhelmed with the lingering effects of our trauma, have felt very distant from God. Terry Gander says,

> There was a time in my life when I denied my faith due to the effects of my combat trauma. Anxiety and depression blocked my faith from aiding in my healing process. This lasted for years. Once I began to heal and partly control the effects of my trauma, I began to regain my faith in God. I began again to read the Bible. I read about the lion and the lamb, which gave me a peaceful feeling inside that I had not felt in years. I knew then that God was by my side to help quell the effects of my trauma.

While feeling overwhelmed during the later life impact of the severe symptoms of my combat trauma, as a chaplain I somehow felt that if my faith had just been strong enough, I would not be experiencing these troubling feelings. I spent time praying about my feelings, but I found this to be hard to do because I didn't want to acknowledge, even in my prayers, how emotionally needy I was in my emotional pain. Plus, my prayers more often than not would turn away from me to that of praying for others. While praying for others was certainly OK, it didn't seem to help me with my immediate pain.

A common question is, "Why do bad things happen to good people? Why are really good guys wounded and killed in the beginning of their prime?" In my counseling, I frequently encountered women who were systematically molested and raped as young girls, usually by a trusted family member. Why does this happen to some girls but not others? Or, why does disease or injury happen to good people? I have no clear-cut answers for these questions. I do, however, know that the Bible speaks of the "rain falling on the just and the unjust."

An answer that I do have from my faith and life experiences is that "any experience can be a good experience, even if it has been a bad experience." God enables me to learn from the bad that happens to me. That does not mean God causes bad to happen. But each human is given the right of self-determination and a degree of freedom to determine what happens in life and the freedom to determine what to do with it.

I can honestly say that I am a much better person because of my entire combat trauma. I more clearly understand the feelings of those who feel the world forced them into the ground floor of a two-story outhouse. As a counselor/therapist, I can more readily identify with the rape victim, the person stricken with a deadly disease, or one who is crippled by a grinding automobile wreck or has a failed relationship.

I do not believe that God placed me in ferocious firefights four decades ago just to "teach" me about life. I do believe that His grace gives me the freedom and insight to better understand the unfortunate who walk near me and more effectively reach out to them in their hurt or dysfunction. Therefore, out of the most dastardly events of my life, good can be and has been the result.

Associating combat trauma with our faith is epitomized for some of us by these words from Terry Gander,

> I'm unique in God's creation; He has made me as I am, as different from other people as the lion is from the lamb. In Christ all differences disappear and my love for others is increased, just like the lion and the lamb. We'll dwell in harmony and peace.

Asking God for understanding, His presence, and His release of us from our awful past goes a long way toward reconciliation with the spiritual parts of our lives.

17

PHYSICAL PROBLEMS AND COMBAT TRAUMA

Heart disease, hypertension, diabetes, intestinal problems, skin disorders, stomach, back, and neck pain, tremors, choking, irregular and fast heartbeat, headaches, and countless other physical problems are exacerbated by systematic and prolonged combat trauma distress. Almost all of us have had a series of health problems over the years. Of course, it is impossible to differentiate between normal problems due to the natural environment and progressive age and that of a lifetime of distress from combat trauma.

Agent Orange has contributed to many of our ailments, although most cannot be proven to have a direct link. The VA recognizes eleven diseases and disorders associated with that horrible chemical. All of us live with the knowledge that the effects of Agent Orange lasts for several generations and thousands of our brothers have already died as a result of Agent Orange exposure. Naturally, the threat of Agent Orange is like a lurking sniper in the tree line that could already have any or all of us in his sights and is just waiting to squeeze the chemical trigger. When one of our brothers goes down from an Agent Orange–related disorder, feelings associated with our combat trauma can quickly resurface.

Many of us have had serious health problems. John Iannucci had a kidney transplant and I lost a kidney due to renal cell carcinoma.

Although not recognized by the VA, there is significant independent medical research that indicates kidney problems can be associated with exposure to Agent Orange. Those of us who were in the infantry in the Mekong Delta were exposed to Agent Orange in three different ways. It was sprayed from the air, the navy sprayed it from boats onto the heavy foliage, and we sloshed through it both in the water and on land.

Many of us have had heart problems, which have included bypass surgeries, stints, and heart attacks. Of course, this is not unusual for men of our ages. Distress from lingering combat trauma can significantly increase the chances of complicating heart problems. Occluded heart vessels can immediately occlude further as a result of a distressful event. When a person dies of a heart attack when seeing a dramatic event such as a wreck or even when excited at a sporting event, more often than not it is the result of quickly restricted blood vessels due to the excitement of the moment.

Therefore, a significant flashback or even a nightmare can have the same effect and we may not even know of the dangers. When my cardiologist learned that I had been diagnosed with and was being treated for PTSD, he strongly demanded that I immediately cease work because, as he stated in his letter to the VA on my behalf,

> the stress associated with his work of counseling coupled with his post traumatic stress disorder results in increased physiologic stress, which does a variety of things, which are counterproductive to his cardiovascular health. By raising his heart rate and blood pressure, it runs the risk of provoking substantial ischemia. Furthermore, stress increases his likelihood for making clots which could lead to pulmonary embolization. . . . His continuing to work presents a significant health hazard and he would be best served by seeking disability.

Numerous physical problems have been encountered by Frank Martinolich, including severe osteoarthritis, degenerative disks in his neck and lower back, mysterious tendon problems, three surgeries on his left knee, total replacement of his left knee, and five surgeries on his right foot and ankle, ultimately resulting in amputation just below the knee. He believes these problems are a direct result of his combat trauma. Taking thousands of steps in and out of calf-deep Mekong Delta mud could very well be a contributing factor in his limb problems.

The terrible battle the night of February 26–27, 1968, made Guy P. Moore think he was going to die. "My stomach hurt so badly from the intense fear of that night that I can still feel it when something is bothering me. I get the exact same feeling that I had that night."

Continual stomach problems are experienced by Bob Stumpf. In June 1998, Bob had abdominal surgery to relieve an acid reflux problem, and his esophagus has permanent damage.

> In the field after hard days of combat operations, it was very necessary to stay awake and alert at night. Being totally exhausted and my body crying for sleep, I remember sucking on C-ration coffee and sugar packets just to stay awake and alert. I go through bouts of diarrhea and am sure most of this is caused by stress and possibly the abuse that my digestive system went through in Vietnam. No wonder my stomach is in such a state today.

Bob also has had angiograms and thallium stress tests because of continued chest pains. Doctors feared blockages but have concluded that the problems are stress related more than physical.

It is common knowledge that distress affects the body. When our nervous system is informed of an immediate danger to our self, the fight-or-flight syndrome kicks in, causing the heart rate to increase and enabling an adrenaline rush to fortify our bodies. Pupils dilate to see better and hearing becomes more acute.

An increasing number of medical researchers are finding physical changes in the brain of victims of prolonged combat trauma as verified by PET scans. Furthermore, research indicates a change in the brain chemistry, the function of the brain, and even in the structure of the brain.

It is also found that during nightmares and flashbacks, the extra release of adrenaline may erode the cardiovascular system, increasing the risk of heart attack and stroke. We can't keep a flashback or nightmare from occurring nor the distress that accompanies them. We can, however, avoid other distressful situations that put us at physical and psychological risk.

As somber as physical problems are to the combat trauma victim, the good news is that through some treatments for trauma, the brain can be retrained and revitalized, reducing some disease risks. If for no other reason, combat trauma victims should seek psychological and medical assistance for these ailments.

18

WANNABES, LIARS, AND PRETENDERS

Many of our brothers have now been dead for four decades, and many other brothers still carry the results of enemy fire with lost limbs, lost eyes, and lost internal organs. The physical scars that many of us have are highlighted by the emotional wounds that are with us every day of our lives—wounds from being in combat almost daily at a time in our young lives when many others were living the "good life," dating, running around at the beach, and going to all-night parties. This we don't resent. But what puts shit in our soda more than anything else are those wannabes who now claim to have been to and done things in combat that are solely in their imagination. Just as bad are the liars and pretenders who tell war stories that are nothing more than bullshit. The woods are full of them, and if we could have our way, they would all be exposed and punished.

An acquaintance of mine was in the army during the Vietnam era but did not go to Vietnam. He was chaptered out of the army. The reason does not matter. But what does matter is that when I saw on his vehicle a "Vietnam Veteran" bumper sticker, I became livid. Even though I did not confront him, I wanted to literally beat the crap out of him. Another acquaintance of mine was actually in Vietnam, but I know for a fact that he served in a support unit. Now, four decades later, this liar has more gory combat stories than he has brain cells. Problem is, none of them are true. Plus, this wannabe wears a baseball cap with the word "Ranger" on it, as if he was a real Ranger. When I am around either of these fakes, I must fight my feelings with vigor to avoid engaging either about their effort to con others about their "combat exploits."

My golf buddy Ray Shurling and I were enjoying a day of golf. Ray was in Special Forces and trained with the famous Son Tay Raiders in Vietnam. Two groups of potential Raiders were prepared to go, but due to security, the team makeup was not disclosed. At the turn, stopping for refreshments, another golfer was giving a line of BS about the Son Tay Raiders, totally unaware of who Ray was or where Ray had been. Ray lost his temper and let this idiot know what he thought of him and his line of lies. For a moment, I thought I might have to pull Ray off this pretender.

Stolen Valor is a book that highlights many in public life who have made claims of combat valor. Yet most of them have not even been in a combat zone, much less been in combat. Words cannot express the absolute contempt that we have for the phonies who now claim "valor" and their claims are nothing but a bunch of lies. Dave Schoenian read the book and says, "I had to read it very slowly as I became very upset. Then I realized I couldn't do anything about them or the people in the VA who beat the system. I just have to take care of me and help my real buddies."

Of course, politicians like Bob Dole, John McCain, Max Cleland, and Bob Kerrey have physical and recorded histories that verify the horror of their combat experiences. However, some others who are quite prominent in public life are decorated, but many of us know for a fact that many of them manipulated the system for future political haymaking.

Another politician actually claimed to have been under sniper fire in Bosnia and had to run for safety. The media immediately proved that this claim just was not so. The excuse given was that "I misspoke" and that the claim was in error due to a busy schedule. If one has actually been under fire, he or she unmistakenly knows it! Bullshitting by any bullshitter makes any combat veteran livid.

Many of our brothers refused Purple Heart awards for "minor" wounds because we didn't think they were warranted when compared to the "real" wounds of our severely wounded brothers. Ray Shurling was once hit in the foot by a fragment from a mortar. However, he refused a Purple Heart, saying, "In my unit, Purple Hearts were not expected for minor injuries of this sort."

To see some politicians four decades later use what many would consider defective awards to manipulate the American public for political gain is to dishonor our fallen brothers. Almost all of us, if using the criteria manipulated by some of the public figures, would be much more heavily decorated, because every one of us did things in battles and received some minor wounds for which nothing was recorded or written up. To those politicians in question, we can only say "Shit happens"—and it stinks!

For anyone to tell a lie about anything else in their lives is none of our business. But to steal the valor of our fallen brothers is a direct insult to our past. If we had our way, to do so would be a criminal offense punishable by prison. Words cannot express how livid it makes us to even hear about any of those fakes and make-believers!

Despite our pain from our combat trauma, we all are glad that we served and take great pride in our past. But as Bob Nichols says,

> Now, it seems everyone wants to be a combat vet. I know two wannabes and have come close to physical contact with each of them. My fear was that if I hit one, I might not be able to stop, they make me so angry. I settle for a few choice words to them.

The Mobile Riverine Force Association, of which many of us are members, has an every-other-year reunion attended by more than fifteen hundred persons. A few years ago, it was discovered that one of the attendees was a wannabe and that he had never even been to Vietnam. When several vets began questioning him about his "unit" and things the unit did, the sorry scoundrel realized he was cornered and quickly departed. He was lucky to have gotten out without some of the brothers taking him outside and giving him an old-fashioned ass-whooping.

A former supply specialist who spent two years in Long Binh with his "Vietnamese family" lived life in a very safe area of Vietnam. Yet, he approached Tony Normand about collecting "his PTSD money"—and, of course, Tony knew this guy was a fake. Tony's label of him is "thief." Tony further adds,

> It just hurts to see those with no valid claim to valor or no experience of having ever been there in the thick of it, or without any deep-seated emotions or personal integrity, besmirch the valor of those who have and do

and will always suffer. I am hurt as they figuratively trample the memory of those who through their sacrifice are not around to make their claim.

Vets who "work the system" with fraudulent claims just to get benefits clog the system. Frank Martinolich says,

I do not have tolerance for liars or cheaters. These fake veterans really piss me off, and what pisses me off more is that they not only get away with it, but there are such weak penalties for them if they get caught. It is amazing how the VA screws legitimate vets, but doesn't try to verify the loser's information. If I overhear someone giving a line of bullshit, I will call them on it. I'm not bashful about that.

Says Roy Moseman:

It seems popular today to be a combat veteran fake, and they are coming out of the woodwork. I can't stand a combat wannabe, pretender, or liar about the Vietnam experience. They are doing an injustice to the brave men and women who fought for this country while many of them stayed home and had a good time. For the veterans who were in Vietnam to lie about what they did is just as bad. Why can't they accept the fact that they were mechanics, cooks, or whatever MOS they had? It doesn't matter. They did their jobs and they all were important. I expect any of us grunts would have been happy to have changed places with them. One truck driver told me how he had killed about eight or ten enemy when his truck wrecked and he had to fight them with his bayonet. He was so full of shit that I came close to kicking his ass on the spot.

Although we all get infuriated at these make-believers, Ron Miriello has somewhat of a compassionate take on them.

The Vietnam wannabes, the pretenders, and the liars are sad people who have no life. They are so lost that they fabricate a life of lies and make-believe and actually start believing their own lies. Rather than hatred or anger, my reaction to their living the lie of "stolen valor" is pity and sorrow.

IV

CARE AND TREATMENT

Living with trauma may not be fun, and our trauma memories will always be with us. However, it is manageable. A trauma victim does not have to sleep under a bridge, stay high, self-isolate, or commit suicide. There is hope and help available. It won't make it all go away, but it can help enable us to better live with our symptoms.

19

REESTABLISHMENT OF
OUR BROTHERHOOD

Imagine a very close family who did everything together: eating, working, playing, sleeping, hoping, praying, laughing—and fighting for our lives. And, then, with no forewarning, the family is suddenly and unexpectedly torn apart and family members are relocated in all parts of the country. This is exactly what happened to us. After living so intimately in daily life-or-death situations, each of us left via medical evacuation or normal rotation home.

Now, imagine there is no way to learn the whereabouts of any of the dislocated family members. The days of tracking persons via the Internet are yet to arrive, and each of us is left with a huge relational gap that is like an open wound that will not heal. This was our brotherhood, a brotherhood that no one can understand except the members of our brotherhood.

Attempting to track down "lost brothers" has become very important for many of us. Paul Harvey made famous the phrase "the rest of the story." With so many of our brothers having been medically evacuated and all the rest of us so young and eager to return to the States, little did we know that several decades later, the relational hole left in our memories would need to be filled. Therefore, many of us have had quests to reconnect with lost brothers for "the rest of the story."

It was 1987. Word spread that the 3/60th was to have a reunion in Colorado Springs. A hotel was contracted and dates set. No one knew who or how many would show up. John Iannucci and wife flew out from Asheville, North Carolina. A hospitality room had been rented. John checked into the hotel, went to his room, and turned on the TV. After a little while, Barbara asked if he wasn't going to the hospitality room. Pretending fatigue, John procrastinated and continued watching the mindless soap on TV.

Likewise, when word reached me about the reunion coming up, I casually mentioned to Barbara that it was going to be held in Colorado. Loving to travel and never having been to Colorado, Barbara assumed I wanted to go and asked for the dates. "Oh, I don't plan to go." I was aware that, strangely, my heart was pounding, but I didn't know why. I just wanted to withdraw. Lovingly, Barbara probed as to why I didn't plan to go. Over the next few hours, for one of the first times in a long while, I was forced to take a closer look inside myself and see the fluttering of my emotions that by now were raging in all directions. After several hours of consideration, I finally said, "OK, I'll go, but only if you agree to go with me." That done, I then said, "And another condition: We'll rent a car and I want you to agree that if at any time I decide we must leave, we leave immediately with no questions asked." Puzzled, Barbara agreed without inquiring about the reasons for this seemingly odd request.

John summoned courage from somewhere deep in his past, perhaps not unlike walking point years prior, and he made his way from his hotel room to the hospitality room. But instead of entering the door, he just kept walking down the hall, aimlessly. The feelings were like sensing an ambush while on patrol and not wanting to walk right into it, so he diverted. Finally, realizing he must, he entered the room. Immediately, he recognized the voice and presence of Will Davis, John's beloved former company commander of Company B. After the first words were spoken, John knew he was finally back home!

At O'Hare Airport in Chicago, as Barbara and I were changing planes, a commotion caught my attention. Four middle-aged guys were hugging and back-slapping in the hallway near the gate. All had on military paraphernalia, and I saw the Ninth Infantry Division patch and a "Wild Ones" tag, which was the 3/60th emblem. Obviously, these four combat brothers were on the way to the reunion and for the first time in twenty years, they were suddenly back together. I observed from a distance, once again with heart pounding and sweaty palms. For some strange reason, I suddenly had the urge to catch the next plane home instead of to Colorado Springs. But, of course, I didn't.

Boarding the plane, I carefully kept my distance, as if the newly reunited brothers had the plague. Refusing to get close to them, clearly I was feeling fear, and it was extremely puzzling.

Upon landing, Barbara and I signed for the rental car, drove to the hotel, and checked in. Shortly, I took a deep breath, walked to the hospitality room and, feeling like I was going into the operating room for exploratory surgery, entered the door. Within fifteen seconds a voice said to me, "Hey, you are Chaplain Johnson, my chaplain!" A second voice boomed, "Chaplain, great to see you! I'm Bravo 6." Surprised, I turned and immediately saw John Iannucci, whom I did not immediately recognize, but I did recognize the black guy with the booming voice as Will Davis, the former company commander of Bravo Company. Within the next ten seconds, as hugs were shared, suddenly twenty years had immediately dissolved and I, too, knew I was finally back home.

This scene was repeated over and over during the following three days as more than sixty members of 3/60th gathered for the first time. It was surreal, as old relationships were renewed and new ones were forged. At the end of the weekend, all the brothers knew that we were home, and our "family" would continue to grow as news of other brothers was exchanged.

This reunion was followed with another one in Florida the next year, and from that, the Mobile Riverine Force Association was formed, which was to include all the units, both army and navy, who fought together in the Mekong Delta. Today, several thousand brothers are members.

But not all the brothers were found immediately. As has been mentioned earlier, some, when found, did not want to reunite with the family because of the painful memories from "back then." But, when a brother is found, there is rejoicing and warm feelings like we have never felt before with any group of persons—not at high school reunions, college reunions, or family-of-origin reunions. Our brotherhood is indeed unique.

The reunion in Colorado for many of us was the first reconnection. Others had been reconnected earlier. John Iannucci first met Dave

Schoenian on a Veterans Day trek to the Vietnam Veterans Memorial Wall. Even though from different battalions, Dave and John immediately knew they were brothers. Dave and Roy Moseman reconnected in similar fashion. Dave and Roy were platoon brothers who were in that terrible battle on August 12–13, 1968, when they took so many losses. They were also on the boat together when the B-40 rocket almost blew Roy's arm off.

It was not until 1999 that Erol Tuzcu learned about the Mobile Riverine Force Association reunions. Attending for the first time, Erol reconnected with many of his long-lost brothers. "When we get together with the brothers at the reunion, the best thing for my soul is to be able to rehash our experiences."

Mitch Perdue read my book shortly after it was published in 2001 and phoned me. A meeting was arranged in Asheville, North Carolina, with Mitch, John Iannucci, and me. Mitch and John were together in that terrible battle of February 26–27, 1968, when only twenty-six brothers walked out. Mitch had similar hesitancy, as did others of us, when he arrived at John's restaurant and we all met for the first time in over thirty years. Mitch says, "As crazy as it sounds, when I arrived at John's restaurant that day, I was scared. I didn't know what to expect."

John Iannucci says,

> My Vietnam friends have played a big part in my life. They are the ones I turn to if I just want to talk, especially if old painful memories have been dredged up. We have a bond that only those who experienced combat can understand. There is a feeling of trust and understanding we have with each other that we don't have with anyone else.

Another time, out of nowhere, the voice on the phone at my home said, "Jim, this is Charlie Taylor from Prescott, Arizona. I was with the 5/60th Infantry in Vietnam with you." With these words from a long-lost and trusted brother, many years were immediately melted as another brother relationship was renewed. Charlie has not missed a Mobile Riverine Force Association reunion since and has been instrumental in establishing 5/60th reunions as well. "At my first reunion, I realized that I was not alone and that the weight I carried for many years was not mine alone. My brothers are more important than ever in my remaining journey through life," Charlie says.

In the mid-1990s, I saw in the paper an article that referenced a Colonel Anthony Normand, the chief of staff of Special Operations Command at nearby Fort Bragg. A phone call confirmed that indeed, this was the Tony Normand from Vietnam, and two more brothers were reunited for "the rest of the story."

A high school civics class invited three other veterans and me to discuss our Vietnam combat experiences. One of the other veterans was Ron Miriello, the navy River Rat from the Delta. Aside from being joint presenters, many additional visits and conversations complete this part of our brotherhood.

Dave Schoenian says,

> One thing people don't understand is how we Nam combat veterans love each other. My wife wishes I would tell her that I love her as often as I do my brothers from Nam. Going to the Vet Center and talking and learning about PTSD, being with men who had and shared the same problems, has made a huge difference in my life. They are now all my brothers, like family. They give me strength to get through the week. I have many pictures of my brothers from Nam, some e-mails, and good memories from the reunions. It's all good and therapeutic for me. I belong to the greatest fraternity in the world, combat veterans of the U.S. armed forces.

Most of us are active participants in our Mobile Riverine Force reunions. Even though many of us served in different combat capacities and in different units and at different times, that does not matter, as we are all brothers and each of us has been and continues to be "welcomed home" by each other.

Terry Gander says,

> The Mobile Riverine Force Association reunions is one place I feel no anger from my experiences in Vietnam because all those attending experienced the same-type trauma. We all have that brotherhood with one another and it is wonderfully soothing for us all. The brothers have experienced the same-type trauma as me and just being with them is salve for my emotional wounds.

Says Frank Martinolich,

> It is impossible to put in to words the feeling of seeing and being with the people you lived and fought alongside. The events we all recalled were

the same, even though all our tours and units didn't exactly mesh. It is a very comfortable feeling. It is amazing to find out the similar problems we all have been experiencing. We just feel safe to be able to talk about our time in Vietnam. A common comment is "That explains a lot of things," when recalling events of the past. There is a visible difference when the information is spoken.

Some of the brothers have been reluctant to reconnect. John Iannucci reached Guy P. Moore about fifteen years ago, and Guy, while respectful, declined an invitation to reconnect. Several years later, he did reconnect and his presence, like all of us, is now very firm. "Only we who have been there really understand. That's the brotherhood I feel at the reunions," says Guy.

Ray Shurling and I began as golfing partners, and a deep bond of brotherhood has developed and remained strong in our brotherhood for many years.

Bob Stumpf has found numerous brothers, and each find has a cathartic impact on him.

This dynamic of reconnecting has happened countless times for many of us, and it always feels so very good. Yes, the brotherhood is unique in so many ways. It has helped us all to know and accept that it really is OK for us to have lived through that hell and it is OK to live now and celebrate life with one another, even if we are still scattered around the country.

(20)

TREATING OURSELVES

Self-help books abound on everything from dieting to parenting to self-esteem. One of the reasons we wanted to share our experiences of combat trauma and its impact on later life is to allow others experiencing similar histories to know there is help available to those who have also been traumatized. It is, we feel, very important to know that there are some things we can and have done ourselves that help. It is not mandatory that one with combat trauma wallow in alcohol, drugs, anger, or anxiety; pace the floor in the middle of the night; or withdraw from loved ones. Yes, feelings are real and our behaviors based on those feelings may seem the only way to react. But it is mandatory to realize that there can be radical, successful, and long-lasting help.

Of course, already mentioned is the reestablishment of the brotherhood. That reestablishment is really like being reborn. We have the power and opportunity to heal ourselves with our brotherhood. As we become "peer therapists," our need for withdrawal or isolation is reduced and our psychological injuries are somewhat normalized. We are not alone.

As is the case with many problems of life, solutions begin to emerge when one admits there is a problem. With the effects of trauma, it took several decades before many of us finally realized we had a problem. The pervasive attitude in the military was, and to some degree still is, that only weak people had or have problems. After getting out of combat, the government's position for years was that combat veterans just need to "suck it up" and go on with their lives. This self-serving attitude did not, of course, help.

One of the most difficult things to do when dealing with the stressors of being back from combat is asking for help. That almost universal initial attitude that "real soldiers" do not ask for help for our unseen feelings did not serve any of us well. In retrospect, that refusal has added untold amounts of psychic pain, not only to us but also to our loved ones. When we were shot or caught a flesh-tearing fragment, we wanted help immediately. Yet, this macho posture kept many of us from acknowledging our need to seek help for our frayed psyches.

Not only was writing a therapeutic agent for me, but in later years my writing helped to qualify and quantify combat experiences and their aftermath for numerous persons who read my book *Combat Chaplain*.

Bob Stumpf says,

> Coming to the realization that something is wrong with the way you think, act and how you view the world and how you respond to your family and friends is a part of what I have learned from the VA and Vet Centers. A combat veteran owes it to himself and his family to seek help if he is having problems.

"It" kept bothering John Adame. "It" had negatively impacted his family relationship, his marriage, job, and friends.

> Finally, I decided "it" was not others, it must be me. I went to see a psychiatrist, who gave me some pills saying they would help. But, they didn't. Two years later, I went to the VA and was placed in a group of forty-two persons. The leader was inexperienced and the group was way too large. The leader lost control of the group and it was apparent that we were not making any progress, so I dropped out. Later, my life was still a mess and I went back a third time. This time, I did one-to-one therapy for four years and as things gradually began coming out, I began getting better.

John became very eager to get a true handle on his problems and he kept trying. In therapy, he was referred to a "Legacy" class, where he began writing his story and these stories were then discussed in class. "Writing has helped me tremendously. I now tell others, 'Write it down. Discuss it with your children and grandchildren. Let them know what you did.'"

Anger and rage are two of the ugly parts of PTSD. Terry Gander says,

> I learned in therapy that my anger is always there, hidden inside me. Keeping my feelings bottled up inside me makes the anger worse. Therefore, I know I need to vent, which quells my anger. The best for me is "keeping a ledger," which enables me to manage my anger instead of it managing me.

Some of the ways we have learned how to deal with our anger include stopping what we are doing when we recognize we are getting angry. Take a walk. Breathe deeply and slowly. Count to ten. Go get a drink of water. Say, "I can handle it. It won't last long." Exercise. Find something to laugh about. Write your feelings. Meditate. The list goes on and on.

Much learning is gleaned from therapy, group meetings, education, developing better coping skills, and treatments from professionals, including cognitive behavior therapy, EMDR, and medicines.

In trying to deal with his combat experiences, John Iannucci read every book, magazine, and newspaper article he could get his hands on. He read religiously every night for many years and eventually collected more than two hundred books. Then he became involved with a local chapter of Vietnam Vets of America. As a group, they make regular visits to Washington, D.C., on Veterans Day to visit the wall.

> My wife and I went to group therapy with other vets and their spouses. I encourage other vets to do likewise, as I am convinced that the best way to deal with our combat experiences is to share them with those who have had the same experiences.
>
> I spend most of my time now living on the outside rather than inside of myself. I found out that the sun shines warmer and brighter outside and my vision for a better future is much cleaner out here.

It has taken a great deal of effort for Tony Normand to lower his shield and share his thoughts on his traumatic distress. Tony confesses,

> Until becoming involved in this writing project, I have never spoken of these events or feelings to anyone. But as I grow older, I have reconciled

my thoughts with reality, forgiven my shortcomings, and laughed at the good times remembered. I am at peace with my soul and with who and what I am. I have learned to endure the nightmares and to even skillfully hide them and what they do to change my moods. It has not been and will never be easy. Still, every once in awhile, I wonder if I have truly learned to live with it at all, or if I am just fooling myself in order to make it all *seem* right. I may never know for sure.

In June 2004, Guy P. Moore attended his first combat PTSD veterans meeting. "After an hour of listening to other combat veterans talk about how combat and trauma had affected their lives, I finally, after thirty-five years, realized that I was not only just like them—I was them."

It is important to remember that the more I know about what is happening to me, the more power I have to manage it. What I think about "it" impacts what happens. No, I cannot control my past, but I can learn to control my reactions and responses to it.

Back then we put a lot of energy into just staying alive. Now, we can learn to live some each day for those who were not as fortunate as us and develop a different respect for life. We can find the good in any situation, regardless of how bad it was. We don't have to dwell on negative talk alone; rather, we can learn positive self-talk by learning to control our inner thoughts and avoid just blaming. We had no control over our environment four decades ago, but we sure as tootin' have many choices now on what we can and will do about our healing.

RETURN TO VIETNAM

The shores of Normandy, American cemeteries in France, and battle sites across Europe and the Pacific have been magnets for World War II vets for many years. Returning to "those places" has proven somewhat of a catharsis for many. We all have visual images of an old veteran in an American cemetery or standing on the shores of Normandy where he and many of his brothers were decimated decades ago.

A part of dealing with our combat trauma involves returning to the "scene of the pain." Four of us felt the pull to return to Vietnam: John Adame, Bob Nichols, John Iannucci, and me. There is a small difference between the concepts of *wanting* to do something and *needing* to do it.

Of course, all four of us also needed to return, and our need was meshed with wanting to do so, as well.

In 1999, John Adame wanted to see "the rest of the story." He traveled in many areas of the Mekong Delta. "I wanted to see how the people live now and see what the countryside looked like without having to be petrified with being ambushed from some tree line." He was able to come to the conclusion that, as bloody as combat was, it was not a personal thing for either us or the enemy.

> They were there to kill me and I was there to kill them. This was our job. As we were riding down the Mekong River, the boat driver asked if I was a vet, and of course, I said I was. "War is over. We are friends, right?" he asked. And, yes the war is over, but I'll always be affected.

Bob Nichols was in a horrible battle on February 20, 1969.

> The enemy got the drop on us and our company commander led us in the wrong direction and we went right into an L-formation ambush. We took many casualties. I can still see many tracers in the dark sky and smell the strong odors. We lost a lot of good men that night, but we also killed many VC.
>
> On my return to Vietnam, one of the places I visited was a VC cemetery in Ben Tre. Numerous graves of enemy KIAs had the date of death of February 20, 1969. It was a strange and sad feeling looking at their graves, knowing that not only did we lose a lot of good men, but many of their "good men" died at my hands as well. I wondered how many of these dead enemy soldiers I killed. In 1969, I probably would have celebrated their death. But, now, it just illustrates that combat is hell, for both sides.

A reunion door prize at the 1995 Mobile Riverine Force Association reunion was free airfare to travel back to Vietnam. My ticket was the winner. Once I decided to return, my buddy John Iannucci asked if he could go back with me.

In 1996, John and I, our wives, and five other veterans returned to Vietnam. We traveled the waterways of the Mekong Delta, found and visited several very significant battle sites, and located some Vietnamese persons we had known. We were able to help fill in some important historical and relational gaps. One battle site we located was of special significance. Following is an account of that battle in Vinh Long on

February 4–5, 1968, which involved me, John, Guy P. Moore, Terry Gander, and John Adame.

The Tet offensive is in high gear. The day after leaving My Tho, Alpha, Bravo, and Echo Company of 3/60th Battalion are suddenly ordered to prepare to fly into Vinh Long to the south. Vietnamese units there are under heavy attack from hundreds of enemy. Our insertion outside the city by chopper is uneventful. Alpha and Bravo companies are adjoined and moving toward a Buddhist pagoda near the edge of the city, while Echo Company is maneuvering about a quarter of a mile across a small stream. It is late afternoon.

We are suddenly ambushed from dug-in enemy in a large cemetery adjacent to the pagoda. We take cover where we can and soon suppress the enemy fire. However, we take several casualties who must be evacuated. A buddy of Guy P. Moore is shot in the chest and is severely wounded.

Night comes and John Iannucci's squad set up in a pigpen. Using starlight scopes, we can see about thirty bodies of slain VC just beyond our perimeter. Throughout the night, Alpha and Bravo receive periodic incoming shells and occasionally small-arms fire, but take no additional casualties.

Echo Company is not so fortunate. About 1:00 a.m., the enemy charge head-on in a frontal attack. Many VC are killed, but as Lt. Ron Wood rises to throw a grenade that kills three enemy, an AK-47 bullet slams into his head. He is dead by the time his body crumples to the ground.

John Adame was a radio operator next to him.

I was in the middle when we were hit. Tracers filled the sky and artillery came on top of the VC for over two hours. We had captured three suspects who were nothing but very young boys. I had been put in charge of them and was told that if we were hit, the three were to be killed. When we were hit, I couldn't bring myself to execute them, so I just crawled to them and cut them loose and they crawled away, all under relentless incoming fire.

During the night, so much artillery was fired that two tubes of 105mm artillery melted. The next morning, after the battle was over, the battalion commander flew in and was in a rage that we had melted the two tubes. My God, we were just happy to be alive after having been so savagely attacked. VC bodies were scattered all over the area, but that didn't satisfy a very angry commander. To this day, I am offended that he did not celebrate that most of us lived through a night of terror, yet he was in a rage that two tubes of artillery had melted. It didn't even seem to matter that one of our lieutenants had just been killed and our entire company had been terrorized all night.

Back across the stream, John Iannucci had spent the terrifying night huddled with his squad in that pigpen. At first light, the firing had stopped and a few civilians began returning to their destroyed hooches. John says,

> I suddenly heard the most heart-wrenching moaning and crying one could imagine. Two middle-aged Vietnamese civilians were in utter shock. Our chaplain, Jim Johnson, went to them and I saw Jim hugging them. Then we saw two oblong piles of ashes. These were the bodies of two old people who obviously had been executed by the VC and burned. The only recognizable parts of their burned bodies were a couple of bones protruding from the ashes.

As the two companies moved out toward Echo Company's position, many enemy bodies and supplies were scattered over the area. A VC body still clutching his rifle was floating in a small stream. In a small pond in front of Echo Company's position were the bodies of several dead VC who were in the frontal assault of the previous night's battle. Most of the soldiers had a glazed look on their faces, as the distress of the past few days was clearly showing on very tired faces.

When John and I returned to Vietnam, we located the very pagoda where the above miserable battle occurred. The cemetery was still there, and our sad memories of our dead brothers along with the Vietnamese who were executed and burned by the enemy were mixed with joy that the war is long since over.

The west bank across the canal from Dong Tam was where we were hit many times. We casually walked among the hooches and residents there and felt tremendous relief that we were not looking for an enemy mortar pit or machine gun position. We later rode through that terrible sea of water, thick underbrush, and leg-sucking mud of the Rung Sat Special Zone. We also went to the Ben Tre cemetery that Bob Nichols visited and had many of his same feelings.

Perhaps the most somber place we visited was the recently opened center that was the equivalent of our Vietnam Memorial Wall. Theirs was indoors and listed the name, residence, and age when killed. We took no joy in the fact that approximately a quarter of a million names are on their wall. Saddest of all was a number of VC killed who were only ten and eleven years old.

Not all Vietnam veterans can or should return to Vietnam. That must remain a personal decision. We can say that there was much cleansing for the four of us. John Iannucci's comment after returning home was, "Vietnam is no longer just a war, it is now a country."

THE WALL

Often called a place of healing and cleansing, the Vietnam Veterans Memorial Wall has become somewhat of a paradox for many Vietnam veterans. Visiting or even thinking of the wall can easily bring back painful memories of brothers killed and of how close all of us came to being killed on many occasions. Some of us have been to the wall numerous times. Others have delayed going, but once having gone, find an almost magical element of humility, reverence, sadness, anger, thankfulness, and even joy in having the surviving brothers that we do have.

Perhaps Charlie Taylor's reflection on his visits to the wall resonates with us all.

It took a long time for me to gather the courage to go to the wall. I first went to the "Moving Wall" in Kansas, but would not let any of my family go with me. Even though my parents, wife, and sons were with me, I had them wait in the van. It was overcast and rainy. It seemed to fit my mood. The emotions were almost more than I could bear. First, there was gut-wrenching sorrow for my brothers I had lost. During my twelve months in C/5/60th, thirty-eight of our brothers were killed, including two of my company commanders and the lieutenant who replaced me when I became the company executive officer.

The second emotion I had was one of anger in wondering if their sacrifice was worth it and anger for the way we combat veterans were reviled when we came home. The ugly truth was, it turned out to not be a particularly good war. Because of political micromanaging, we won our battles but were not allowed to win the war. We were not welcomed back and there was no heroes parade.

Finally, on a business trip to Washington, I went to the wall. Two business associates who were Vietnam vets went with me, for I needed their support. The first time, I went at night because I was embarrassed for others to see my tears and anguish. During that trip to Washington, I went to the wall a total of three times; I could not stay away.

On the plane home, I started reading the book *Shrapnel in the Heart*. I alternated between racking sobs and being embarrassed and then not caring what other travelers around me thought. Each sob seemed to reduce the heaviness of my psyche, and that was the start of my healing and letting go of the burdens I had been carrying.

The next step in my healing came at my first reunion. I realized that I was not alone and that the weight I fought with for all these years was not mine alone. My brothers are more important than ever in my remaining journey through life.

Bob Stumpf says,

The wall is my constant companion. I have visited there many times with some of my brothers who have been a major part of helping me with this lifetime struggle with PTSD. When I read the names of all the brothers that I served with, I grieve for all that they lost. I grieve for all the wonderful things life gives to us that they never were able to experience. I grieve for the families who have lived with such pain and loss. Sometime my own pain gets so great that my emotions shut down. It is like I am looking at the wall through a third person. It's not too unlike it was four decades ago when the pain and losses were too much for my soul to bear and I had no time or opportunity to grieve. When I look at the wall, I still see the images of our buddies getting hit, of loading poncho-covered brothers onto the choppers for their long ride home. None of this will ever cease for me until I have joined them. Not a day goes by that I don't mourn the losses.

Roy Moseman says,

I have been making a Veterans Day trip to the wall for about fifteen years. I love to visit the wall very late at night, sometimes as late as one or two in the morning. It is so quiet and peaceful at that time. I don't have to wade through the crowds. I can find the names of the men that I served with and just peacefully remember them. I often wonder why their names are on the wall and not mine. I wonder what they would be doing today if they had made it home. It's a place that in my mind I can go back to

1968 and remember them as they were and to make peace with them and myself. I seldom visit the wall that tears do not flow as I step in front of that black wall.

My wife, Barbara, strongly encouraged me to go to the wall during a trip to Washington. To appease her, I consented to go. I describe my visit in my book this way:

> I think I can just walk by, but I discover I can not. By the time I'm halfway down the slight decline with the wall on my left, I'm absorbed with the entire environment. It's like the wall has tentacles that reach out and pull me in. I slowly focus on some names, no name in particular, just several names. I understand that each name represents a life that is no longer; a life wasted. I meander for awhile. Barbara graciously allows me time and space, no idle chitchat. I'm oblivious to other visitors. It's like all the years come together for me at this very spot. It's time to leave, and I'm surprised to discover that I'm crying. I'm shocked at the emotional impact just walking by this black granite wall has on me. I'm just profoundly sad. I'm not ashamed of my tears, but I'm mystified at how quickly my feelings have surfaced.

The wall is the one place where we the living come face to face with our dead brothers. It's more than a visit to a cemetery. It is the symbolism of where our misery four decades ago is intermingled with our brothers killed in action, whom we will never forget. For us who made it out, it is a wall of honor as well as a celebration of lives lost and still living.

21

THE VETERANS ADMINISTRATION

Thankfully, today the VA is considerably more progressive and active in offering treatment and assistance to veterans than it was in years past. We certainly know that the VA system, both medically and administratively, has been stretched, and this no doubt has created delays and in some cases degraded service and treatment. Most of us, though, have seen significant positive changes in recent years, and we are grateful.

The early years after Vietnam were lost years, in that the VA system was anything but user friendly. After Vietnam, if you had been combat injured, you could count on being treated. But if you had emotional wounds, many were given the message "You are a bother." Medical treatment of all kinds has drastically improved over the past decade or so. In fact, signs of kindness are seen on medical center walls, stating "It is now our turn to serve you."

The VA cannot be of help until the vet recognizes there is a problem. Taking care of oneself and getting help is key to being able to deal with the explosion of emotions that frequently occur.

"Something is wrong with me" is a conclusion that many of us delayed acknowledging for much of our life. How could "something" not be wrong with us? No way is it normal for a young man, barely out of high school, to be exposed to all the trauma and terror of constant combat and to not have been severely damaged emotionally.

When Dave Schoenian first went to the VA, he went with some guilt, because "I felt that being a true warrior you didn't show signs of weakness. I felt an unseen anxiety and imagined peer pressure from other vets. Somehow, I thought you didn't go to the VA unless you had both legs blown off." Dave had his first Compensation and Pension hearing on September 11, 2001. He was basically denied the first go-round. However, he decided to appeal and they gave him another hearing.

> With the help of a veteran's service officer, I got started and did most of the work on my own. I had to gather and provide evidence. I worked with a guy who was going through it himself, and he coached me. I listened to the guys at my group, read all I could, and prepared my case like a lawyer would. My advice is not to give up and get discouraged because I believe the system is made difficult in order to get one discouraged. It actually took me about two years to go from zero to full benefits. It was worth it, because now the VA has given me any and all the treatment I have asked for.

Terry Gander feels, "Now that PTSD has been recognized by the VA, many vets are receiving medical care not previously available. I honestly do not think I would have made it through to this time in my life without the proper care and treatment. For this, I am extremely grateful."

VET CENTERS

After a divorce, Frank Martinolich started private therapy. His intent was to try to find out why he was attracted to certain types of women. After his first session, the therapist said she thought he had PTSD.

> Of course I thought that was just plain bullshit. I didn't know much about it, but I was sure I didn't have it. She tested me and verified I did have PTSD, but I still denied it. In 2003, I finally found my way to the Vet Center, had one-on-one therapy for a while, and went into an anger management class. I then was placed in a focus group. We are able to talk about what has been going on in our lives and then discuss it. We actively support each other. I still go the Vet Center every other week.

It took many years for Bob Stumpf to come to terms with why he was feeling and acting the way he was.

> The Vet Center has been a place of safety for me. The people who work there are dedicated to us. This place has become a godsend. There is such a comfort to know that all generations of vets who have experienced catastrophic combat experiences can now receive help. I know I will never be free of my PTSD, but after four decades, I have gotten a portion of my life back by finding different ways to cope, thanks to the Vet Center.

VA CLAIMS SYSTEM

The VA claims system has improved but still has a long way to go and needs much improvement. There seems to be no consistent standard of rating procedure. What is proper in one district is not proper in another district. There is clear evidence from internal investigations in the past that some raters actually see themselves as adversaries to veterans. If a claim can be minimized, then the government has saved money, regardless of the need of the veteran. Just recently, the press exposed an official e-mail from a high-level staff person who stated in essence that PTSD diagnosis was becoming too prevalent and offered ways to delay and deflect ratings in order to save the government money. Nevertheless, the system offers advocates for veterans and an appeal process that seems much fairer than in the past.

It is important to know that it is up to the veteran to prove his case. "But it's all in my records" is not sufficient to support a claim, as the reviewing officer is not going to dig into one's records. Doing that is the responsibility of the vet himself—i.e., to extract the mitigating records and present those as necessary evidence in a claim. Likewise, supporting documents and support letters are very important, but again, it is the vet who has the responsibility to engineer his case. Be tenacious in pursuing your claim. Submitting a claim to the VA is not unlike going to court as the plaintiff. It is your responsibility to prove your case because the reviewing officer is like a judge who only has access to what the vet presents as evidence.

Roy Moseman says,

> I had a problem with the VA when I first filed for PTSD. They first gave
> me 30 percent disability. At first I accepted it and then I decided to ap-
> peal. It took over a year of filing and mailing papers back and forth. I saw
> a private psychologist who specialized in PTSD and a VA psychologist
> who had been a navy corpsman in Vietnam, and both knew what I was
> dealing with.

He was successful with his appeal.

No system is perfect. Even with flaws, we feel that the Vet Centers
and VA medical facilities are a wonderful effort of our government to
provide for veterans' sacrifices, and we are grateful.

INPATIENT PTSD TREATMENT

Outpatient group and individual therapy is very important. However,
the VA has a number of inpatient treatment programs where a veteran
can get more intense therapy for PTSD.

In July 2005, Guy P. Moore had been having suicidal ideations and
was feeling very hopeless.

> I had no desire to live any longer. After twenty-nine years of marriage, my
> wife, Joann, knew me pretty well. She begged me to please give inpatient
> treatment a chance. I really did not think I could learn how to live a better
> and happier life, but I was soon proven very wrong. Out of desperation,
> I entered the North Chicago VA Medical Center combat trauma unit for
> five weeks, and I can truly say that these five weeks were the most produc-
> tive weeks of my entire life.

After Guy had been in treatment for three weeks, he was able to take
a weekend leave home to Detroit. Joann was absolutely floored at the
kinds of change she saw in her husband. "He was an entirely different
man and his outlook was drastically changed. They saved Guy's life."

Guy had been in combat from day one in Vietnam. In his inpatient
treatment, he quickly learned that he was suffering from a multitude
of postcombat distresses, which included recurrent and distressing

thoughts/memories, dreams, and nightmares of Vietnam; isolation and avoidance; emotional numbness; no sense of future; survivor guilt; sleep problems; anger and rage; difficulty focusing, concentrating, and remembering; hypervigilance; exaggerated startle response; panic attacks; headaches and stomach problems attributed to anxiety; major depression; and low self-esteem and self-worth.

I went to North Chicago believing it was my last hope; and it gave me hope. I know PTSD cannot be cured, but it can be managed and controlled. There is no magic pill, but medications do help. I learned in treatment that:

1. I need to challenge myself to socialize with others.
2. Meditate on pleasant things.
3. Every morning I have a little alone time and I say to myself, "Today is going to be a great day, and if something comes up that is not to my liking, I am going to deal with it with intelligence and not as a crazed animal."
4. React or respond? Every time someone says something to me that just might piss me off, I try to stop and ask myself what is this asshole trying to say. Looking at it from that person's point of view keeps me from getting upset, mad, or violent.
5. Death: When I think of my friends who died in combat, I naturally tend to get sad, depressed, and mad. Knowing that this is not good for my mental health, I try to switch my thinking to the fun times we had together. I dwell on their smiles, the sounds of their voices, and try to avoid thinking of the way they died. They are not gone forever, because in my mind, they live.

In January 2003 Bob Stumpf was placed in a twenty-six-day PTSD program at the Batavia, New York, VA Medical Center.

This program was a catharsis for me. Even though I will always have these problems, the Batavia program helped me to understand and define what was and still is going on in my life. They taught me coping skills, gave me the knowledge, and made me feel safe in an environment and place that I never knew existed. For this I will always be grateful. Then, after the October 2005 reunion, where we honored Joe Rees and I met his family, I left feeling like a huge emotional chunk had been taken out of me. I had been to many reunions, but this was the first time I ever left feeling so depressed. No doubt it was due to my unmourned memories of my buddy, Joe. I went back to Batavia for another week. That was a parachute for me and a safety net. I have found my safe haven.

In 2005, when I was at the height of overwhelming resurgence of feelings from Vietnam, Bob Stumpf strongly encouraged me to enter the Batavia, New York, inpatient program. As I considered it, Guy P. Moore also talked to me about his experience with inpatient treatment at the North Chicago VA and also encouraged me to get into treatment. One of the best things I have ever done for myself is to follow Bob's and Guy's advice. I probably would have never sought this type of treatment if they had not reached out and encouraged me.

Also having been referred to a seven-week program in Hilo, Hawaii, Frank Martinolich was exposed to anger management, self-medication, substance abuse, social interaction, childhood autobiography, military training, combat trauma, and postmilitary life.

Inpatient treatment is not for everyone, nor can everyone take the amount of time for this type of treatment. However, the VA has come a very long way from the early days when the bureaucracy just wanted vets to go home and shut up to these days of having programs of education and treatment for the combat-traumatized veteran.

22

VETERANS HELPING VETERANS

"Veterans helping veterans" is the motto of Dave Schoenian and most of us. The biggest help to a veteran is to assure him that it is proper to ask questions and get help if needed. Equally important is to care for one another.

Not knowing one has PTSD causes suffering in ways that a combat veteran should never have to experience. Fortunately, we have been able to help others by reaching out. Dave says,

> I didn't even notice the effects of my trauma, but two Vietnam vets I worked with did. They stiff-armed me to get me to the local Vet Center. In doing so, they literally have saved my life. I was in terrible shape and did not even know it. This was in 2001. I began going to the VA in Pittsburgh and started seeing a psychiatrist. I go to group therapy each Thursday night and I do not miss a meeting if at all possible. Yes, building a trust in the guys took some time, but now I know that I cannot do without it. Now, these guys are my brothers and we are indeed family. I'll go to these sessions the rest of my life.

Ron Miriello is a regular presenter at a local high school and his college as he shares the effects of his combat.

> I feel strongly that helping others is what best helps me. I have developed a very effective PowerPoint presentation that allows me to not just share

experiences and opinions, but also to teach people about the Vietnam War. Though I become emotional and hyper during each and every presentation and it is difficult for me, I have extreme difficulty saying no when asked to present. Again and again, audience members, both young and old, often share that the knowledge gained during this single presentation, "exceeds all I've ever known or learned about Vietnam."

Many of those who hear Ron's presentations have family members who are combat veterans. By understanding the reality of combat from Ron's perspective, these people can help the veterans in their own families.

Taps at funerals for deceased veterans is a very moving and meaningful part. Bob Nichols volunteers his time as an accomplished bugler for playing taps.

Roy Moseman says,

I have talked to a lot of guys from my old unit and to any other veteran that I run into who I think I can help. It's not something to be ashamed of, and if they have trouble with the results of their combat trauma, like I have, then I think they surely deserve to be helped. I have received so much support from my friend Dave Schoenian. We were in the same squad in Vietnam and were beside each other on the night of that awful battle of August 12, 1968. We both understand each other and can freely talk about our feelings.

Being in the elite Special Forces and airborne created a "super stud" ideation for guys like Ray Shurling. He resisted even going to the VA for years.

Fortunately, my best friend, Jim Johnson, recognized that I had many symptoms of PTSD and was privy to some of my behaviors. He encouraged me to get help with my trauma symptoms, but I kept delaying it. Finally, I took a deep breath and lowered my guard and did it. I received a rating of 70 percent and now I cannot understand why I was so reluctant to ask for help.

On a drive to the beach for vacation, Mitch Perdue began reading my book and decided to phone me. After a few moments, I mentioned that one of Mitch's company members from Vietnam, John Iannucci, lives an hour away from him. It was agreed that the three of us—John, Mitch, and I—would meet at John's restaurant. Mitch says, "Arriving at the restaurant, I was anxious yet eager to connect with these two brothers. Now, I am so glad I did." As a result, Mitch has helped many other combat veterans.

Mitch believes that God keeps sending Vietnam vets to him for help.

> Recently, I took a vet to the VA for the very first time to get his VA card. I accidentally met him in a grocery store and learned that he has all the symptoms of PTSD. He is all but illiterate and had no clue of how to get help. We talked long about his situation. It feels good to know that this vet, who is sixty years old, is finally getting the help that he so desperately needed.

Another vet named John is very sick with cancer and has numerous combat-related problems. Yet, John had never been to the VA and was building heavy debts for medical care. When Mitch learned about his needs, he was very instrumental in this vet getting a VA rating. Even though he is terminally ill, at least he will be able to get some back compensation that his wife can use to pay some of his bills. Additionally, Mitch was instrumental in having a major fund-raiser for John. Mind you, this was a total stranger to Mitch until they met accidentally. Yet, they were combat brothers.

Recently, Mitch was visiting a family member in the hospital and he accidentally met another vet. While they were there, a medical helicopter flew in bringing a patient from a wreck. Both Mitch and the other vet were on the verge of having a flashback and began talking about their experiences. Many feelings came out of the other vet as a result of the chopper, because it was so like a medevac chopper from Vietnam. He had never talked about his experiences to anyone, and he and Mitch talked beyond midnight.

Dave Schoenian says,

> I make it my job to help other vets and guide them in any way I can. This makes me feel good, seeing those who deserve VA help finally getting it. However, I am very picky about who I help. If their answers to my questions don't mesh properly, then I don't extend myself because there are still too many "make-believers" and bullshitters who are just trying to work the system.

As already mentioned, some veterans are still too emotionally wounded to be receptive to help. A number of years ago, John Iannucci phoned Guy P. Moore. While cordial, Guy declined John's invitation to attend an upcoming unit reunion, and it was not until more than ten years later that Guy decided to contact John. This set in motion Guy's being able to reconnect to many other veterans, as well as being of tremendous help to others who need Guy's care.

John, who has owned his restaurant for many years, often hosts veterans passing through the area. John's generosity of time and food is legendary among hundreds of veterans.

For all of my adult life, being a helper, caregiver, nurturer, counselor, and therapist was not only what I did for a living, but it was my life. Especially after my book was published, hundreds of veterans from all over the country contacted me, often just to talk—because, as many of them said, "I finally have found someone who knows what combat was like and can understand what I went through." However, gradually, I began to spiral down and roles were reversed, in that my trauma symptoms were beginning to weigh very heavily on me and interfered with my life in many ways.

For the first time in my life, because of the reassociation of my brothers from the Mekong Delta, they began to reach out to me. At one of the reunions, I mentioned to Bob Stumpf that I was having a difficult time. Being intuitive, in the months ahead, Bob contacted me several times and encouraged me to go to inpatient treatment at the Batavia, New York, VA Medical Center, which is where he went. At the same time, I was having some physical problems and Roy Moseman phoned me with encouragement. Also in my corner and strongly supporting and encouraging me were John Iannucci, Terry Gander, Mitch Perdue, and Dave Schoenian. They saw my needs when I didn't. These guys will never know how valuable they were at times when I was feeling very low. The fact that I can now help other vets is directly due to their care for me.

Inmates at San Quentin State Prison in California who were Vietnam veterans somehow got a copy of my book and passed it around. Together, they requested of the prison administration that if at all possible, could this guy (me) come and spend some time with them. Upon receiving an official invitation from the warden, Barbara and I traveled from North Carolina to California and visited the thirty-one inmates there who were Vietnam veterans. We spent several days interacting with those imprisoned veterans. The interaction was dynamic and Barbara and I, as we left, agreed that a combat veteran's needs are the same, whether a local neighbor or a convicted felon in San Quentin who may never see the light of day outside the prison walls.

More recently, the North Carolina Center for Death Penalty Litigation requested I connect with three combat veterans on death row, which I did. Even though they were guilty of some terrible crimes, I spent numerous hours with these condemned prisoners simply as one veteran trying to help another veteran.

We cannot change the horrors of combat four decades ago nor the residual emotional impact of our terror that exists today. But we can reach out to other veterans because helping others is hopefully helpful to them and equally healing to us, the helpers.

23

THEN AND NOW—AGAIN

The message, then, about combat trauma is essentially the same regardless of the specific war or details of the terror experienced in combat. Our messages are these:

To the combat veteran from past wars: It is indeed OK to feel what you feel. Your feelings do not make you crazy. Even though it may have been many years since your combat experiences, your feelings are what they are. Don't deny them. You are not alone, so don't stay alone. Reach out—to your loved ones, to the Vet Center, and/or the VA. Help is available. Talk to your children about your combat experiences, and if you can't talk about it yet, write it for them. They'll love you for it.

To more recent veterans of trauma from Afghanistan and Iraq: Take advantage of help offered to you from the military and the VA. Don't resist your hot lines and after-combat screenings. There is nothing wrong with your feeling what you feel.

To loved ones: Your combat veteran family member may have a wounded soul that you cannot fix. However, you can listen without judgment, nurture him or her, and assure the veteran that your love is unconditional.

To the American public at large: Please do not look at us as crippled. Please do see us as perhaps having wounded souls. Combat trauma may be indeed a mental illness, but more importantly it is a *combat wound to the soul.*

To clinical providers: Thank you for helping us. You may not understand our behaviors, but neither do we. Without you, who knows where any of us would be?

To our national leaders: Even though combat is often a necessity, when young men and women are sent into combat, please do not forsake us when the shooting stops. Please consider the longer-lasting effects of decisions to engage our enemies. Those of us who are wounded in combat, physically and emotionally, did what you asked us to do, and that was to go into combat. Please, please, do not ever shun and marginalize us again.

To those other trauma victims who have been traumatized in noncombat situations such as wrecks, rape, abuse, and natural disasters: Please know that you are not alone.

Even though the military still has a macho image and some prejudice against troops who are traumatized, the environment is changing. Just recently, a two-star general from the reserves and a four-star commander, General Carter Ham, sought screening for combat stress after returning home from Iraq in 2005.

Yes, combat trauma is horrible. Yet we all have unique ways in which we experienced the trauma then and now. We can't change the past, but we can manage our feelings and behaviors—and that is exactly what all sixteen of us are trying to do.

And, yes, the combat environment has changed over the years. The difference from how the War for Independence and the War between the States were fought to the present is dramatic. Today, troops have the ability to phone home, e-mail constantly, usually return home with their units, and have usually had less sustained combat than in past wars. Nevertheless, as already said, trauma is ever present from roadside bombs, snipers, suicide bombers, and so on.

Our message to the hundreds of thousands of veterans, family members, friends, neighbors, coworkers, and health care provides is that, yes, life goes on. But it is so much better when we can understand and be understood and can nurture and be nurtured through our historical hurts.

Bob Stumpf's message to new combat veterans is this:

One of the hardest things to do when dealing with the stressors of coming home from combat is asking for help. Coming to the realization that something is wrong with the way you think, act, feel, and view the world and how you respond to your family and friends is a heads-up to get some help. You owe it to yourself and your families to seek help at the vet centers and VA hospitals.

We sixteen sincerely thank you for listening to our stories.

IN MEMORIAM: MITCHELL PERDUE

November 12, 1946—September 9, 2009

It felt like another brother was killed in combat. But, this time, instead of an enemy's bullet, it was cancer that killed our brother, Mitch Perdue. He lived less than nine months after the cancer was discovered. As mentioned earlier in these writings, every man should have a spouse as dedicated as Mitch's wife, Debra, who was with him every step of his final journey.

It was fitting that we had his memorial service at Fort Jackson, South Carolina, hosted by the namesake of our battalion in Vietnam, the 3/60th Infantry Regiment, which is now a basic training unit. This is where Mitch took his basic training. This is also where his father, a World War II veteran, received his training.

Tributes to Mitch came from far and wide. They include the following:

> Mitch Perdue is my hero, not only for what he did as a young soldier in Vietnam, but also for what he did with his life afterwards. I will miss him terribly.

> —John Iannucci, Asheville, North Carolina

Mitch was such a kind gentleman and the most caring person I knew. He and I served together in Vietnam. He left such an impact on the people he met.

—Lance Peterson, Maple Grove, Minnesota

Mitch was one of my heroes. He was great in our platoon in Nam. I felt very safe with him near me. He was absolutely dependable for everything and anything.

—Jim "Doc" Parker, Huntington, West Virginia

A fellow brother in arms. . . . As you were blessed, so were we to have him as a member of our unit.

—Rodney Berkey, New Port Richey, Florida

He will always be remembered and missed by all of us combat brothers in Bravo Company.

—Guy P. Moore, Saugatuck, Michigan

Mitch has the love of all his Ninth Infantry Division brothers with him.

—Jace Johnston, Scottsdale, Arizona

I knew that I could depend on Mitch in a tight spot. It is a great honor to have served with him.

—SSG Larry Reed, Watauga, Texas

Another sad day has come to the men of Bravo Company. I know that he shall be waiting with open arms when it is time for his brothers-in-arms to join him.

—John Sperry, Sodus, New York

It has been my joy and privilege sharing days at chemotherapy with Mitchell. He gave so much of himself to everyone he met and never asked for anything in return.

—Bonnie Hodges, North Augusta, South Carolina

He was a jolly, kind, and thoughtful man who filled each day with happiness and a little mischief.

—Kathy and Ryker Hall, Richmond, Georgia

He shared more love and sunshine in the last few months of his life than most of us do in our entire lifetime.

—Nancy and Tim Owen, sister and brother-in-law

Mitch had a fighting spirit, infectious laughter, and had nothing but goodwill to all he called friend or family. To have been his friend meant "for life," no matter what.

—Mary Ann, Benson, Eliza, and Elliott Bagwell,
Clemson, South Carolina

Til the end of your battle with cancer, it was you who lifted us in our most desperate times. Your faith was unyielding. Your passion for living will live on in us. You inspired us by your strength, faith, and love of your family.

—Nieces Lisa Molinowski and Paige Dillon

You are the life of the party. I love you more than my heart.

—Madison Cheek, granddaughter, age 9

You are the sweetest, most loving, funniest Papa in the entire world and you are my hero. What you and I do best is go to breakfast at McDonald's, ride the golf cart, and feed the ducks. You mean the world to me!

—Kodi Cheek, grandson, age 13

We are so incredibly blessed to have shared this journey with our compassionate, brilliant, jolly, and inspirational father. *He is truly our hero*!

—Daddy's girls, daughters Crystal Cheek
and Lauren Perdue

A few days prior to his death, Mitch and I shared some reflections of our lives' journey. We both knew he only had a very short time to live. With all his family at his bedside, we laughed, reminisced, and made an agreement that, whichever of us got to heaven first would find a peaceful "heavenly" stream. When the second arrives, we will gather on the quiet streambanks with our other combat brothers and share the peace of eternity—but with no enemy snipers, booby traps, ambushes, gunboats, choppers, C rations, or that god-awful leg-sucking mud.

Yes, Mitchell Perdue was loved and respected, and we know our lives are richer for having known him. Until we meet again, may God rest your soul. . . .

INDEX

161; lifetime sentence, 4, 167, 171, 173; macho is hindrance, 109, 160, 182; management, 5, 162, 173; news reports, 13; peer therapists, 159; psychological injury, 4, 12; return visits to Vietnam, 34, 162–66; secondhand PTSD, 135, 137; self-help, 159; sharing with others, 161; symptoms, 14; thousand-yard stare, 36; unseen combat wound, 12–13; untreated, 136; writing as therapy, 160; vets are not alone, 14. *See also* Veterans Administration (VA); Vet Centers
punji pits, 20

racing thoughts, 97
radio operator, 60, 115, 118, 164
Raulston, Lt. Grayson, 26
recoilless rifle, 21, 52
Rees, Joseph, 32, 173
reunions of the brotherhood, 157–58, 167; Colorado Springs, 3/60th 1967, 154; fear, 155; Mobile Riverine Force Association reunion (1995), 163; not want to reunite, 155; 5/60th, 156
river rats, 8, 10, 21–23, 113, 157
road runner operations, 59, 87, 112
rocket propelled grenade (RPG), 20–25, 55, 58, 115
rockets, 25
Rung Sat Special Zone, 111, 127, 165

Saigon desk jockey, 29
Saigon, 59
San Quentin State Prison, 178
Scheyer, Bob, 15
Schoenian, Dave, 9, 27–28, 30, 42, 47, 62, 72, 77, 84, 89, 94, 96,

101, 109, 116, 119, 122, 125–26, 129–30, 135, 139, 148, 156, 170, 175, 177–78
Schoenian, Ella, 62, 129, 135
"It don't mean shit," 35–36, 77
Sholty, Don, 26
"short timer" calendar, 36
Shrapnel in the Heart, 167
Shurling, David, 97
Shurling, Debbie, 108
Shurling, Ray, 10, 14, 32, 42–43, 52, 61–62, 67–70, 77, 79, 84, 94–95, 103–5, 107–8, 117–18, 124, 126, 137–39, 148, 157, 176
sleep, 45–46; helpless, 58; lack of, 57, 122, 130; medications for, 63; nightmares, 3–4, 31, 36, 42, 45–47, 56–57, 61–63, 69, 75, 130–31, 145, 162; night sweats, 57, 61–63; paralyzing, 57; racing mind, 61; under bridge, 46; violent dreams, 57, 62
Son Tay Raiders, 148
Special Forces, 10, 33, 108, 138, 148, 176
Special Operations Command, 9, 126, 159
startled, 95–96; by engine backfire, 95; by quick movements, 95
street people, 84, 127
Stumpf, Bob, 10, 21, 32, 42, 48, 63, 73, 77, 79–80, 84, 89, 97, 100–1, 104, 106, 109, 112, 119, 122–23, 126, 129–30, 132, 137, 145, 157, 160, 167, 171, 173–74, 178, 182
Stumpf, Mary, 137
snipers, 20, 55, 60, 95, 122, 182
Snoopy's Nose, 23, 58, 117. *See also* battles
suicide, 5, 9, 31, 46, 128, 136, 151, 172

ABOUT THE AUTHOR

James D. Johnson retired from the army as a lieutenant colonel (chaplain). He is also retired as a pastoral, marriage, and family therapist. He has a *doctorate in marriage and family* from Eastern Baptist Theological Seminary (now Palmer Theological Seminary), a master of science from Long Island University, a master of divinity from Southeastern Baptist Theological Seminary, and bachelor of arts in religion from Wake Forest University. He has earned three Bronze Stars, an Air Medal, five Meritorious Service medals, two Army Commendation medals, and nine other national and foreign military awards. He is the author of *Combat Chaplain: A Thirty-Year Vietnam Battle*.